Cost-Value Analysis in Health Care

Making Sense out of QALYs

This book is a comprehensive and fully up-to-date account of what it means to try to quantify health in distributing resources for health care. It offers an elegant new approach to the costs and the benefits of medical interventions.

Cost-Utility Analysis (CUA) is a method designed by economists to help decision makers distribute scarce resources to areas of health care where they will yield the greatest benefits. A core element of CUA is the use of data on patients' quality of life to weigh life years spent in different states of illness relative to years spent in full health. Erik Nord questions the feasibility of measuring patients' quality of life meaningfully in numerical terms, as CUA presupposes. He presents an alternative approach, called cost-value analysis, in which representative samples of the general public express preferences among health-care programs that differ with respect to the number of patients who are targeted, how ill they are, and how much they will benefit from treatment.

This book will be of particular interest to medical ethicists, health-care professionals and administrators, and economists specializing in health economics.

"Among the strengths of the book are its excellent exposition and its success in raising insightful and crucially important issues, making a major contribution to ongoing debates." – Amartya Sen

Erik Nord is Senior Researcher at the National Institute of Public Health, Oslo, Norway.

Cambridge Studies in Philosophy and Public Policy

General Editor: Douglas MacLean, *University of Maryland, Baltimore County*

Cost-Value Analysis in Health Care

Making Sense out of QALYs

ERIK NORD

National Institute of Public Health, Oslo, Norway

CAMBRIDGE
UNIVERSITY PRESS

PUBLISHED BY THE PRESS SYNDICATE OF THE UNIVERSITY OF CAMBRIDGE
The Pitt Building, Trumpington Street, Cambridge, United Kingdom

CAMBRIDGE UNIVERSITY PRESS
The Edinburgh Building, Cambridge CB2 2RU, UK   http://www.cup.cam.ac.uk
40 West 20th Street, New York, NY 10011-4211, USA   http://www.cup.org
10 Stamford Road, Oakleigh, Melbourne 3166, Australia
Ruiz de Alarcón 13, 28014 Madrid, Spain

© Erik Nord 1999

First published 1999

Printed in the United States of America

Typeface Palatino 10/12 pt.   *System* DeskTopPro$_{/UX}$®   [BV]

*A catalog record for this book is available from
the British Library.*

Library of Congress Cataloging-in-Publication Data
Nord, Erik, 1948–
Cost-value analysis in health care : making sense out of QALYs /
Erik Nord.
p.   cm. – (Cambridge studies in philosophy and public policy)
Includes bibliographical references and index.
ISBN 0-521-64308-2 (hbk.). – ISBN 0-521-64434-8 (pbk.)
1. Health care rationing.   2. Medical care – Cost effectiveness –
Mathematical models.   3. Quality of life.   4. Life expectancy.
I. Title.   II. Series.
RA410.5.N67   1999
361.1–dc21   99-11394
CIP

ISBN 0 521 64308 2 hardback
ISBN 0 521 64434 8 paperback

For Nora and Even

Contents

Contents

Contents

Tables and Figures

TABLES

FIGURES

Preface and Acknowledgments

I remember that when I first heard about the Quality Adjusted Life Year (QALY) I thought it was a good idea. After all, we do want to do as much good as possible with the limited resources available for health care, don't we? And doing good through health care does involve precisely what QALYs purport to encapsulate: reducing symptoms, improving functioning, and prolonging life.

Ten years later I still like to say that the QALY has an intuitive appeal as a measure of benefit. But I must add that economists and others advocating its use in informing decisions have no reason to be proud of the way in which they have raised their baby. At the age of twenty-five, it remains much the same simple construct as it was at birth, in spite of countless suggestions from its surroundings that a fair amount of socialization and sophistication would be needed for the baby to become an accepted and respected member of the community.

In this book I first explain the rationale of economic evaluation in health care and the problem that QALYs purport to resolve in such evaluation. I then address a number of issues related to the value basis of QALYs and the particular way in which the concept of QALYs is operationalized in mainstream health economic analysis. The aim of these sections is to shed critical light on the meaning and validity of the numbers that are presently being produced and used in the field. I proceed to propose a particular way of looking at those numbers that make them meaningful and to suggest what they roughly should look like in order to reflect society's structure of concern in resource allocation in health care. In doing so I implicitly adopt the position that it is possible to model societal, ethical preferences for resource allocation in numerical terms. Not everybody will agree with this. But even if such modeling is feasible, there remains the question of whether decision makers will find the numbers useful as aids to real-life decision making. This issue is addressed in the last section of the book.

I am grateful to Dan Wikler of the University of Wisconsin at Madison, whose idea it was that I should try to write this book. Going further back, I am indebted to Alan Williams at the University of York, England, who invited me into this research field ten years ago and never stopped listening, even after I started becoming difficult. I owe thanks to colleagues Ivar Sønbø Kristiansen, Jan Abel Olsen, Paul Dolan, and José-Luis Pinto for their friendship and sharing of professional interests over many years; to Jeff Richardson at the Centre for Health Program Evaluation in Melbourne, Australia, and to Paul Menzel at the Department of Philosophy, Pacific Lutheran University, Tacoma, Washington, both of whom have been enthusiastic friends and invaluable discussion partners and have profoundly helped me to clarify my thinking both before and during the writing of the present volume.

I particularly want to thank Jeff Richardson, with whom I worked very closely on a number of empirical investigations in Australia. Jeff and I have published several articles from this collaborative work, and the reader will see that I draw heavily on these publications in the present book.

Lastly, I would like to thank Alan Garber, Emmett Keeler, and Jon Magnussen for offering helpful suggestions in earlier versions of the manuscript. If unclarities remain, it is certainly not the fault of any of them.

Most of the manuscript was written in the course of a four-month leave from the National Institute of Public Health in Oslo, spent partly at the Center for European Studies at Stanford University and partly at RAND, Santa Monica, California, with financial support from the Norwegian Research Council. I am very grateful to all four institutions for the opportunity they gave me to work in pleasant, peaceful surroundings. I am particularly grateful to Arild Bjørndal and Ivar Sønbø Kristiansen for helping me obtain my leave; to Henrietta Grant-Peterkin for receiving me so wonderfully at Stanford, including helping me retrieve all the baggage that remained at Heathrow; to Inger Anne Landsem, Jon Magnussen, Ane, and Mari for sharing family life with me in Palo Alto, and to Shan Cretin, Emmett Keeler, Whitney

Green, Bob Brooke, Audrey Burnam, Ron Hays, and a number of colleagues at RAND for receiving me so hospitably in Santa Monica.

I am indebted to Marili Juell, whose assistance in Oslo with both professional and private matters I could not have done without, and whose many newsfaxes made Norway feel a lot less far away.

Lastly I thank Nora, who waited so patiently back home, and Even, my buddy in Santa Monica.

E. N.
Oslo, May 1999

Overview

There is general agreement that a health-care insurance scheme, be it public or private, should not aim to provide all the care its members might want. Rather, it should try to be *as valuable as possible* to its members, given the resources these members have made available. This is the same as saying that it should give priority to activities that have a favorable ratio between benefits and costs. In that way it will maximize the membership value, hereafter called the *societal value*, of health care.

A number of approaches are available for estimating the societal value of health interventions at a numerical level. This book focuses on *cost-utility analysis*, which is a special variant of cost-effectiveness analysis. It uses the concept of a Quality Adjusted Life Year (QALY) to overcome the problem of comparing outcomes that are different in kind. In this approach, any state of illness or disability may be assigned a utility on a scale from zero (the utility assigned to the state of being dead) to unity (the utility assigned to being in full health). The value of a health outcome for an individual is calculated as a product of two factors: the increase in the utility of the person's health state as measured on the 0–1 scale and the number of years the person gets to enjoy this improvement. The measurement of outcomes in terms of QALYs in theory allows for comparisons of cost-effectiveness ratios across all kinds of conditions and interventions and also for the calculation of the total societal value of different health plans.

Historically, constructors of the QALY approach have assumed that societal value is a simple, unweighted sum of individual health benefits, in other words, that society disregards how a given total amount of benefits are distributed across people. This is referred to as the assumption of *distributive neutrality*. While there is increasing recognition among advocates of the QALY approach that this assumption is probably *not quite true*, there is little realization that it could in fact be *very wrong*. I argue in Chapter 4 that the assumption violates – in part strongly – a number of societal concerns for fairness in the allocation of health-care resources. First, it overlooks the strength with which people wish to give priority to the severely ill over the less severely ill at the expense of the total amount of health produced. Here the empirical evidence is substantial and suggests dramatic errors in existing instruments for assigning utilities to health states for resource allocation purposes. Second, the QALY approach overlooks a societal concern to allow people to realize their potential for health, whether this is big or small. This implies less discrimination than is suggested by the QALY approach between groups of patients with different capacities to benefit from a given treatment. One aspect of this is that it seems unethical to assign more value to extending the lives of healthy people than those of disabled people. Concerns for the realization of potentials for health are also well documented with respect to improvements in functioning and quality of life for people with nonfatal illnesses. Data furthermore suggest that the QALY assumption of proportionality or close-to-proportionality between duration of benefits (related to life expectancy) and societal value is exaggerated. Third, it is unclear whether the strength with which the QALY model assigns more value to treating the young than the elderly is consistent with societal preferences when concerns for both duration and fairness are taken into account. Fourth, the QALY assumption of proportionality between the number of people treated and societal value is exaggerated.

On the basis of these observations I contend that to rank projects in terms of costs-per-QALY as often as not may tend to distort resource allocation decisions rather than to inform and aid them.

Technically it is feasible to multiply individual utility gains by societal equity weights in order to incorporate concerns for fairness in QALY calculations. However, this presupposes that the measurement of individual utilities in itself can be conducted in a satisfactory way. In Chapter 5 I question this. I judge procedures for measuring utility in the light of four requirements: that utilities be evidence-based, at a cardinal level of measurement, conceptually understandable, and empirically verifiable. Given these requirements I reach the following conclusions.

QALY calculations purport to capture what actually comes out of different health interventions. Utilities for use in QALY calculations should therefore be measured ex post. Aversion to risk and time preference need to be incorporated in a societal ex ante value function for health care programs in terms of separate discount factors.

Ex post utilities should be based on patients' self reports rather than on people's valuation of hypothetical health states with which they have limited direct experience.

It is not sufficient to elicit utilities by means of rating scales, because responses on such scales do not have the necessary cardinal scale properties.

To be understandable and verifiable to potential users, utility numbers need to be interpreted as values assigned to life years in different states rather than as measures of feelings of wellness.

Given this interpretation, both the standard gamble and the time trade-off yield verifiable numbers. But time trade-off utilities are preferable to standard gamble utilities, because they have a much simpler empirical interpretation and therefore are far easier to understand.

So, when a curious potential user of utility numbers asks what a utility number U for a health state A actually stands for, I suggest that the researcher answer that it is the time in full health (expressed as a fraction of a year) that is considered as valuable as a full year in state A, judged ex post by a person in state A. By choosing this interpretation and the measurement procedures that go with it, the researcher may ensure that the utility number is evidence-based, has cardinal properties, and is understandable and verifiable.

However, the QALY algorithm presupposes that in all states of illness there is a trade-off to be made between gains in quality of life and length of life. If QALYs are interpreted as measures of psychophysical quantities, then such a trade-off exists by definition. But when this interpretation is rejected in favor of one in terms of individuals' valuations, it becomes an empirical question whether people really are prepared to make such quality/quantity trade-offs under all circumstances. I argue that in two circumstances they are not. These are, on the one hand, when services lead to minor functional improvements and, on the other hand, when patients face life-saving procedures – in other words, services at the two ends of a societal value continuum for health services. In neither of these situations can we expect to observe a quality/quantity trade-off. I conclude that if QALYs are to be understood as a sum of individual valuations of health benefits, then, contrary to its basic intentions, the approach is not applicable across the whole range of health-care interventions. To achieve such overall applicability, QALYs would need to be based on societal valuations of health-care programs rather than on individuals' valuations of health benefits for themselves. This requires a different technique for valuing outcomes than those presently being used in the field.

In Chapter 6, I recommend the person trade-off technique for valuing outcomes from a societal perspective. The rationale for this is simple. The purpose of assigning numerical values to health outcomes is to establish the trade-offs that society wishes to make between competing programs or projects that – due to differences with respect to costs per person treated – include different numbers of persons. The purpose, in other words, is to establish person trade-offs on the value side that are comparable to person trade-offs on the production side (the latter showing up in the cost data). The intuitively natural valuation technique is then direct person trade-off questions. In these, the researcher specifies the characteristics of outcomes of different kinds and seeks representative samples of the general population to express the number of people obtaining one kind of outcome that they would regard as equivalent to a given number of people obtaining another kind of outcome. I present a set of values for health states that is based on extensive international research using the person trade-off technique and other supporting observations. The set of values purports to encapsulate societal concerns, not only for utility production in health care, but also for giving priority to the severely ill over the less severely ill, and for not discriminating too strongly against people who happen to have lesser potentials for health than others. I also suggest that the use of health state values be restricted so as to allow for the equal valuation of life-extending programs for healthy and disabled people. The values may be used to calculate cost-effectiveness ratios comparable to those in use today; however, I suggest they be called *cost-value ratios* because of their wider meaning. I finally discuss some of the possibilities and limitations for the use of such ratios in practical decision making.

Reader's Guide

This book is meant for practicing health professionals, health administrators, and politicians as well as for academics working with cost-effectiveness analysis and QALYs. While it offers a simple explanation of the rationale and use of economics and QALYs in informing resource allocation decisions, it also gives a comprehensive critique and reinterpretation. In some parts it thus raises issues of considerable technical complexity.

The practically oriented reader will gain most by concentrating on Chapters 1–4, the section on "whom to ask" in Chapter 5, Chapter 6, and the example of cost-value analysis given in the Annex. The untrained reader may want to save the discussion of "the quantity-of-wellness interpretation and value interpretation of utility" in Chapter 5 for a later occasion.

Chapter 1

Maximizing Value in Health Care

1.1 INTRODUCTION

This book is about the potential use of a numerical economic evaluation model called the QALY (Quality Adjusted Life Year) model in
setting priorities in insurance plans for health care. Such plans may be
either public or private. The former are tax-financed. They generally
aim at providing access to necessary health care to all members of
society regardless of their income. People who elect to have such
schemes do so out of a combination of self-interest and a desire to
help fellow members of society who happen to fall ill. Public schemes
include national health services in countries all over the world, as well
as, for instance, the Medicaid system in America. Private insurance
plans are financed by premiums paid either directly by individual
members of the plans or by the individuals' employers. Membership
is voluntary and motivated by self-interest. In the United States the
majority of health insurance is privately financed, whereas in most
other countries private plans are supplementary to a national health
service.

The point of both public and private insurance plans is to have
members prepay for statistically predictable consumption of health
care. Copayments made by patients at the point of consumption of
health care are small or nonexistent. With such a payment arrange-
ment, patients will tend to demand even such services as are of little
or modest value simply because it costs them very little to do so.
However, members of insurance plans are not interested in having
their money spent on covering low-value services for other people.
Nor do they consider it important for themselves to be insured in such
a way as to receive such services free of charge. They are mainly

interested in being part of an insurance plan that covers *important* health needs, particularly important needs that are costly to accommodate.

In recognition of these preferences, there is general agreement that a health-care insurance plan, be it public or private, should not aim to provide all the care that its members might want. Rather, it should strive to be *as valuable as possible* to its members given the resources that these members have made available. This is the same as saying that it should give priority to activities that have a favorable ratio between benefits and costs. For brevity, I shall hence forth refer to this aim as *maximizing membership value*. When other writers speak about "societal values" in health care (see, e.g., Gold et al. 1996), it is usually such "membership value" to which they effectively are referring. To accord with common parlance, I shall in many places use the term "societal value" synonymously with "membership value" (exploiting the fact that societies can also be private). The question being studied in the book is whether a numerical economic evaluation model can aid administrators of public and private health insurance plans in maximizing membership or societal value. By "administrators" I mean, then, doctors in administrative positions, health bureaucrats, and health politicians.

1.2 THE RATIONALE FOR NUMERICAL MEASURES OF VALUE

A necessary (but not sufficient) condition for judging whether or not membership value is maximized is knowledge of which factors affect people's valuations of different health-care activities. This may vary across communities. However, from public debate in recent years on priority setting in health care in countries such as Holland, New Zealand, Norway, Sweden, and the United States, the following have emerged as potentially significant determinants of value:

1. The number of people helped by the activity.
2. The severity of the patient's condition in terms of loss of quality of life
3. The degree to which the service reduces symptoms and improves functioning
4. The degree to which the service increases the patient's subjectively perceived quality of life

5. The number of years the patient gets to enjoy improved health and/or quality of life (including increased life expectancy)
6. The age of the patient
7. The distance in time until the gain in health materializes (future gains may be valued less than present ones)
8. The patient's responsibility for his/her own illness
9. The patient's responsibility for caring for others
10. The effect of care on a patient's productivity

Factors like sex, race, education, and income, on the other hand, have generally been deemed irrelevant to determining the value of health outcomes.

To be able to maximize membership value, health insurance administrators further need to know the relative importance that members attach to these various factors. Governments in Norway (Norwegian Priority Committee 1987), Holland (Dutch Committee on Choices in Health Care 1992), New Zealand (Campbell and Gillett 1993) and Sweden (Swedish Health Care and Medical Priorities Commission 1993) have chosen to lay out this information in terms of *verbal guidelines for priority setting*. For instance, the Norwegian government, with the approval of Parliament, stated that the most important criterion for prioritizing among patients is the severity of the patient's state of illness, subject to the condition that effective treatment is available, whereas, for instance, the patient's age and responsibility for his own illness were explicitly classified as being of little importance. In our terminology, this is the same as saying that the most valued activities in the Norwegian National Health Service are those which help the most severely ill, and that, for example, heart operations provided to seventy-year-old smokers and to fifty-year-old nonsmokers are regarded as equally valuable.

Although verbal guidelines may be helpful to decision makers, they lack precision. For instance, the Norwegian guidelines suggest that treating a few severely ill people is regarded as just as valuable as treating a considerably greater number of moderately ill people. But how much greater is "a considerably greater number of people"? It could probably mean anything from five times as many to a hundred times as many. Now assume that, in a given decision situation, the cost of treating one severely ill person were having to refrain from treating fifty moderately ill people. It would then be difficult to tell, on the basis of the *verbal* guideline, whether or not the greater value

3

of treating the severely ill person was sufficient to justify the opportunity cost (i.e., the failure to treat the fifty moderately ill people).

It therefore seems quite sensible and legitimate to ask whether it is possible to elicit preferences from members of health insurance plans in a way that would allow decision makers to estimate the value of different health-care activities more accurately, that is, in terms of numbers. This is precisely what health economists are trying to achieve.

The problematic part of this effort is, of course, whether it really is possible to represent complex value judgments in numbers that are sufficiently on target – not only to be helpful to decision makers but to be more helpful than verbal guidelines. In other words, how well can such numbers predict the choices that members of insurance schemes would make if they were asked directly to rank, in terms of value, different ways of using a given amount of resources? To what degree are there biases in these predictions; and to what degree do they have random error? These are the crucial questions we need to address when evaluating numerical models for assessing the value of health-care services.

1.3 AVAILABLE NUMERICAL MEASURES OF VALUE

A number of approaches are available for estimating the societal value of health interventions at a numerical level. I review them briefly here. Later I shall present in greater detail the approach that is the focus of this book, namely cost-utility analysis based on the concept of the Quality Adjusted Life Year (QALY).

In *cost-effectiveness analysis (CEA)* in the original narrow sense, health outcomes are expressed in *natural units* such as number of cases of disease prevented, number of lives saved, or number of life years gained. Such measurements are useful in comparing alternative programs the outcomes of which are similar in kind – for instance, programs all of which lead mainly to the prevention of premature deaths. The attractiveness of CEA lies precisely in its use of natural outcome units, which most people can easily understand and intuitively accept as measures of value. Its weakness lies in the inability of the approach to allow comparisons of programs having outcomes that are different in kind – for instance, programs that lead to different kinds of functional improvements or symptom relief. The measurement of value in terms of natural outcome units hence does not allow for a calculation of the total value of a health insurance scheme that covers life-extending procedures as well as a wide range of health-improving procedures.

Cost-utility analysis is a special variant of cost-effectiveness analysis. It uses the concept of a QALY to overcome the problem of comparing outcomes that are different in kind. In this approach, any state of illness or disability may be assigned a numerical score reflecting the *utility* – that is, the goodness – of the state to the individual concerned. Utility is expressed on a scale from zero (the utility assigned to the state of being dead) to unity (the utility assigned to being in full health). The value of a health outcome for an individual is calculated as a product of two factors: the increase in the utility of the person's state of health as measured on the 0–1 scale, and the number of years the person gets to enjoy this improvement. The measurement of outcomes in terms of QALYs in theory allows comparisons of cost-effectiveness ratios across all kinds of conditions and interventions, and also permits calculation of the total membership value of different health plans.

In *cost-benefit analysis (CBA)* the value of different health outcomes is measured in terms of subjects' willingness to pay to obtain the various outcomes in question. An advantage with this approach is that it allows comparisons not only of health outcomes that are different in kind (as the QALY approach does) but also comparisons of health outcomes with other goods and services. It therefore has the potential to inform decisions regarding the allocation of resources to health care as opposed to other areas of consumption. The QALY approach does not allow this, inasmuch as health care is the only area in which QALYs are used as a measure of value.

There are a number of problems associated with measuring people's willingness to pay for health care (Olsen 1997). This may be a reason why cost-benefit analysis has played a modest role in health economics hitherto. However, further research may draw more interest to this approach in the future (Johannesson and Jönsson 1991).

The World Health Organisation is organizing a large international collaborative enterprise called the *Global Burden of Disease Project* (Murray and Lopez 1996). The idea behind the project is to aid priority setting in health care at the global level by collecting statistics on the degree to which different diseases represent a burden to mankind in terms of the number of people affected, life years lost, and losses in quality of life. Burden of disease is estimated by assigning disability weights to different kinds of illness. The weights use the same 0–1 value scale as the QALY approach, except that the scale is turned around, so that zero represents "no burden" and unity, "maximum burden" (equivalent to "as bad as being dead"). The weights are used in combination with age weights to translate individual life scenarios into a number of Disability Adjusted Life Years (DALYs).

Apart from the age weighting, DALYs are conceptually equivalent to QALYs, inasmuch as they combine reductions in morbidity and mortality in a single value index. However, disability weights for DALY calculations are, since 1995, based on a procedure for preference measurement that is quite different from those used in the QALY field. An important part of the criticism of QALYs presented in this book therefore does not apply to DALYs. On the other hand, there are other problems with DALYs that are worth looking into more closely. I briefly discuss what I perceive as a major problem in the final chapter. For an extensive discussion of DALYs, readers are referred to Anand and Hansson (1997) and Murray and Acharya (1997).

In the following chapters I focus on cost-utility analysis. I show that a policy of maximizing health gains in terms of QALYs disregards highly significant societal concerns for fairness in health care. The QALY approach furthermore uses the concept of cardinal individual utility, which is not only difficult to measure in an understandable and verifiable way, but also unnecessary to measure when the ultimate goal is to estimate *society's* valuation of health-care outcomes. I suggest a model for such valuation that differs from most existing models for QALY calculations in that it compresses mild and moderate states of illness to the upper end of the 0–1 value scale. The result is that severity of illness receives much greater weight in the assignment of value, and discrimination against patient groups with lesser potentials for health is significantly reduced. The model also restricts the use of health-state values so as to allow for the equal valuation of life-extending programs for healthy and disabled people. I suggest *cost-value analysis* as a suitable name for this approach.

Before I go into the details of QALYs, I wish to make three basic points, which the reader should keep in mind throughout the rest of the book, concerning the need to distinguish between different decision contexts in health care and what priority setting in health care essentially is about.

Chapter 2

Three Basic Issues in Economic Evaluation

2.1 AT WHICH LEVELS OF DECISION MAY ECONOMIC EVALUATION BE HELPFUL?

There are, broadly speaking, three levels of decisions at which the goal of maximizing membership value may be pursued. One involves decisions that determine the capacity to admit patients with different conditions or the capacity to implement different preventive programs (including, e.g., screening programs). This is the *budget level*. Another consists of decisions regarding which individuals to admit to a service, given the capacity to treat which has been decided for that service. This is the *admission level*. A third comprises decisions about how to treat those individuals who are admitted. This is the *bedside level*. At each of these levels alternative courses of action may be judged in terms of costs and benefits. In other words, they are all decision levels that in principle lend themselves to economic analysis. On the other hand, the psychological circumstances surrounding resource allocation decisions vary considerably across these levels. Budget decisions concern people who are unknown to the decision makers (so called statistical patients). The decisions are made by many individuals together in a lengthy process in which there is room for careful analysis in a written form. By contrast, decisions at the bedside level are made by a single doctor or a small team of doctors who face their patients directly and often are quite pressed for time. Decisions at the admission level lie somewhere between these two extremes, particularly with respect to the degree of personal contact between patients and doctors. Given these varying circumstances, many will argue that formal economic analysis has a role to play primarily at the budget level of decision making. *This is also the perspective that I adopt when I go on to discuss the relevance of economic analysis.* I shall touch on the application of economic analysis at other decision levels only briefly in the final chapter of the book.

2.2 VALUES WHEN CARING FOR OTHERS VERSUS VALUES WHEN THINKING ABOUT SELF-INTEREST

At the budget level, there is a need to distinguish between two different perspectives in which the values of members of health insurance schemes may be studied. One is particularly relevant when administrators in a national health service are to decide how a given budget should be distributed across specific programs and diagnostic groups that are asking for resources. If, to aid the health service administrators, a representative sample of the population is asked how they think the budget should be spent, most people in the sample will be people in normal health who will not themselves be benefiting from the expenditure, whatever distribution is decided. Their responses will therefore mainly reflect what they think is an efficient and at the same time fair way to distribute health care to fellow citizens in need. I call this the *caring-for-others perspective.*

A different perspective is relevant when administrators in a private insurance scheme are to decide which procedures to include in the scheme and which to leave out. If, to aid the administrators, a representative sample of members of the plan are asked to state their preferences, most people presumably will think about their personal long-term interests and answer accordingly. Such self-interest may have two kinds of basis. Some members will be aware of their own existing or likely future health problems and will express strong preferences for the inclusion of treatments for these specific problems. However, most members will have quite limited knowledge of their own future health-care needs. Behind such a "veil of ignorance" (Harsanyi 1953; Rawls 1971) a member, when asked whether a procedure X should be included in the insurance plan rather than a procedure Y, would need to consider how highly he (or she) would value receiving this procedure if he happened to need it relative to how highly he would value receiving procedure Y if in need of that. I call this the *self-interest perspective.*

The caring-for-others perspective has relatively little relevance for decision making in private health insurance plans, inasmuch as people elect to establish and join such plans instead of public ones not out of concern for others but rather out of self-interest. On the other hand, the self-interest perspective, while most easily recognized in a private insurance context, is highly relevant also in a public health service. A public service makes many decisions that determine the availability of different procedures in the long term – for instance, decisions not to offer certain procedures because they are deemed to be of little value relative to their cost. Such decisions may affect anybody sooner or later. The self-interest perspective behind a veil of ignorance – along with the caring-for-others perspective – therefore seems relevant in informing those decisions.

Arguably, self-interest judgments behind a veil of ignorance subsume judgments about efficiency and fairness in caring for others. The argument goes like this: If people personally think it is more important to be able to receive a given treatment if they happen to get illness X than to be able to receive another given treatment if they happen to get illness Y, then they will also consider it right to give priority to people with illness X over people with illness Y.

At first glance, this is a compelling argument. On the basis of it one might argue that the self-interest perspective behind a veil of ignorance is really the overriding perspective in both the public and the private decision context described above. However, I believe this argument is flawed both at the theoretical and the practical level. In theory, it is perfectly possible to hold independent ethical concerns in addition to personal, "selfish" preferences when choosing from behind a veil of ignorance among different options in resource allocation.

To see this, consider for instance two interventions for patient groups A and B, respectively. Patients A are initially at a functional level that we may call "very severely disabled," while patients B are at a somewhat higher level that we may call "severely disabled." Treatment of patients A will help modestly and take them to the initial level of patients B (severely disabled). Treatment of patients B is highly effective and will take them all the way to full health. Assume that the two illnesses in question occur equally frequently, and that the interventions cost the same. Imagine that there is room for including only one of these two interventions in a public health insurance plan. An individual asked to express his preference from behind a veil of ignorance about his own future health could in theory take the following position. Personally, he would like to maximize his expected health gains from the public health service. Were he only to think about himself, he would therefore vote for the inclusion of the intervention for patients B, since this intervention provides a health gain that seems more significant.

However, the two alternatives have different consequences with respect to the overall distribution of health in the population. Assume that there are one thousand people in each of patient groups A and B in a particular year. If patients A are included in the public health plan while patients B are left untreated, the result will be that all two thousand patients will end up as "severely disabled." If only patients B are included in the plan, one thousand patients (B) will end up healthy, whereas another thousand (A) will remain "very severely disabled." In other words, the inclusion of patients B would lead to a more uneven distribution of health than the inclusion of patients A. The individual whose preferences are being asked could feel uncomfortable with this distributive consequence. He could also feel an obligation to give priority to those who are worse off to begin with. These are ethical concerns (rather than concerns for efficiency). On the basis of such concerns he might vote for the inclusion of A rather than B despite his personal preference for maximizing expected health gains when benefiting from the system himself.

The belief that the self-interest perspective from behind a veil of ignorance could completely override the caring-for-others perspective is probably untenable also at the practical level. When budget decisions are made in real life, nobody is behind a veil of ignorance. It is inevitable that people, when making judgments concerning others, let themselves be influenced by emotions stirred by the specific characteristics of the allocation options presented (e.g., that the disease in question occurred in one's one family). It is not to be expected that the preferences following from these emotions should entirely coincide with long-term preferences expressed in cool, neutral circumstances behind a veil of ignorance.

Some will regard these emotions as factors that distort rational preferences and feel that their influence on resource allocation decisions should be minimized. As argued by Menzel (1990), one way to do this would be to have members of health insurance plans *precommit* health administrators – and thereby give *prior consent* – to adhere strictly to values established behind a veil of ignorance when making budget decisions. Knowing that they had given such prior consent, members would theoretically be more prepared to control their emotions in given budget decision situations.

Again, this is an ideal, theoretical point. In real political life, I think there are limited possibilities for precommiting members of the public to accept resource allocation decisions that intuitively are felt as unfair at the moment of decision. This is most easily seen in public rescue situations, for instance, when identified individuals are trapped in a mine or well or collapsed building, or are reported missing in the wild or at sea, and where actions to save them are extremely costly. It seems unlikely that any kind of prior social contract could stop people from feeling a strong obligation to do everything possible to save the endangered individuals and hence from supporting necessary expenditure to do so. This is what is known as the Rule of Rescue (Jonsen 1986). It is a particularly strong mechanism when identified individuals are in great need. But the same psychology, although not as pronounced, also manifests itself, for example, in annual budget decision-making processes. I believe this is to some extent an unavoidable fact of political life with which health-care decision makers will always have to live. Public health insurance schemes that aim at maximizing membership value therefore need to take into account not only values as they appear in a long-term self-interest perspective behind a veil of ignorance, but also concerns for fairness as expressed in a caring-for-others perspective "in front of" the veil of ignorance.

In summary, people may adopt two perspectives when asked about preferences for resource allocation in health care. One has to do with self-interest, the other with concerns for fairness when caring for others. Figure 1 summarizes the role of these perspectives in various decision contexts.

The fact that preferences can be examined in two perspectives complicates the writing of this book. The exposition will easily become cumbersome, and perhaps confusing, if throughout the text I examine different parts of the QALY model first within one perspective and then within the other. I shall therefore choose one perspective as the main framework and then, at certain junctures, make additional comments with reference to the other.

It is not clear from the literature which of the two perspectives health economists have in mind when they write about QALYs. However, in more recent years a number of writers have discussed the trade-off between efficiency and equity in health-care (Culyer 1991; Wagstaff 1991; Williams 1997). The interest in the notion of equity

Figure 1. *Self-interest and ethical concerns in different decision contexts*

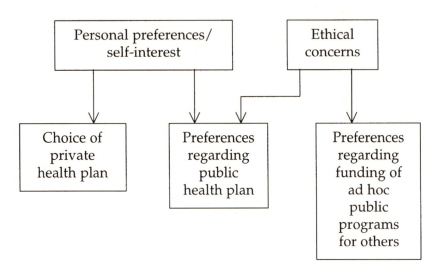

suggests a moral perspective that goes beyond stimulating the pursuit of self-interest only. This is consistent with the point made above that ethical concerns may be held independently of personal preferences and may modify the preferences for social choice that pure self-interest would suggest.

The perspective that I have chosen as the main one is the caring-for-others perspective. One reason is that values held in this perspective de facto are highly relevant in informing budget decision making in countries with national health services – that is, the vast majority of developed countries. Second, most of the evidence on public preferences for resource allocation in health care has been collected within a caring-for-others perspective. At present, in other words, empirical testing of the QALY model, which is a main aim of this book, is primarily possible within this perspective. Third, as noted above, to show interest in the caring-for-others perspective is not inconsistent with mainstream health economics. In Chapter 3, however, I will present some data that shed light on the validity of the QALY approach in modeling societal preferences in a perspective of self-interest behind a veil of ignorance.

2.3 RESOURCE ALLOCATION ACROSS PROGRAMS IS ESSENTIALLY ABOUT MAKING PERSON TRADE-OFFS

The QALY approach to prioritizing in health care derives from fundamental principles of welfare economics. The principles are briefly explained in the appendix to this chapter. In health care, the principles take on a specific form, involving the concept of *person trade-offs*. Before looking closer at the QALY approach, it is essential that the reader appreciate the significance of this concept in resource allocation at the budget level of decision making.

Consider a health insurance scheme with one million members that receives an increase in its total budget of one million dollars per year. Two categories of patients with conditions A and B respectively are suggested as contenders for these additional resources. The cost per patient treated is 1,000 and 10,000 dollars, respectively. This means that if the additional resources are used to include patients A in the scheme, 1,000 patients will be treated per year. If, instead, the resources are spent on patients B, 100 patients will be treated per year. In other words, the ratio of 1:10 between the costs per treatment implies a trade-off between the number of people treated of 10:1. We may call this *the person trade-off on the production side* between patient categories A and B.

Thus, choosing to spend a given amount of resources on a number of patients of one kind is to trade off specific numbers of patients of other kinds who also could have used those resources. In general economic jargon, this is the *opportunity cost*, or the *marginal rate of transformation in production* (see appendix to this chapter). In health care, opportunity costs and marginal rates of transformation are essentially person trade-offs.

In the example above, the question that the health insurance administrators need to address is whether the value of treating each patient of type B is so much greater than the value of treating each patient of type A that it could justify trading off the treatment of ten As for every single B treated. In other words, is the treatment of one B as valuable as the treatment of ten As? *This is the same as saying that health insurance administrators need to compare the person trade-off on the production side with the person trade-off on the value side.* That is the essence of their decision problem. (The point is a special case of a general theorem in welfare economics, namely, that to optimize resource allocation, marginal rates of transformation in production need to be compared with marginal rates of substitution in consumption; see appendix to this chapter).

Bearing in mind that the aim of a health insurance scheme is to maximize membership value, let us see how the person trade-off problem in the example above looks in the self-interest perspective. Behind a veil of ignorance about own future health-care needs, if category A patients are included in the insurance scheme, the value to each member will be a chance of one thousand in a million of receiving treatment for condition A in any given year. So, in statistical terms, the expected value is 0.001 times the value of treatment A. If, instead, category B patients are included in the scheme, the value to each member will be a chance of a hundred in a million of receiving treatment for condition B. The expected value is then 0.0001 times the value of treatment B. This is what Paul Menzel calls "the QALY bargain" (Menzel 1990). To maximize membership value, members must decide which of these two options they prefer. That choice may be seen as a choice in terms of probabilities. But the *material choice* is really between two courses of action that involve different numbers of persons treated: Considering the consequences in terms of expected benefit for yourself (and others, in a public insurance scheme), do you think the additional resources should be used to include a thousand persons of category A or a hundred of category B? *Like the health insurance administrators, insurance scheme members are essentially faced with a person trade-off problem, and it is the person trade-off judgments of these members that the administrators ideally should compare with the person trade-offs on the production side (the cost data).*

In practical economic analysis, the person trade-offs on the production side and the value side between two health outcomes A and B are compared implicitly by comparing the *cost-effectiveness ratios* of the two outcomes. Assume, for instance, that, at the margin, the unit production cost of A is 1,000 dollars and its value – in terms of consumers' willingness to pay for it – 5,000 dollars. The cost-effectiveness ratio is then 1,000:5,000, or five dollars of value per dollar of cost. Assume similarly that the cost-effectiveness ratio of B is 10,000:30,000, namely, three dollars of value per dollar of cost. A then has a better cost-effectiveness ratio than B. This is a direct reflection of the relationship between the person trade-offs on the cost side and the value side. Ten outcomes of type A can be produced for each outcome of type Y (unit costs are 1,000 and 10,000 dollars respectively). At the same time, it only takes six outcomes of type X to compensate for one outcome of type Y in terms of value (values are 5,000 and 30,000 dollars respectively). So, in moving resources from B to A, the person trade-off on the cost side (PTO-C) exceeds the person trade-off on the value side (PTO-V), and this is precisely what shows up in the cost-effectiveness ratios. If the two person trade-offs were equal, the cost-effectiveness ratios would also be equal. If PTO-C were lower than PTO-V, then the cost-effectiveness ratio of A would be lower than the cost-effectiveness ratio of B.

Person trade-offs on the production side are given by the relative costs of treatment. The great challenge in health economic evaluation is to assign values to health outcomes that reflect person trade-offs on the value side. If this can be done, a potentially useful *guideline* to decision makers emerges: In choosing between two or more ways of using a given amount of resources, give priority to that use which has the better cost-effectiveness ratio.

How, then, can administrators get a picture of members' person trade-off judgments on the value side? Health economics suggests that such a picture may be provided by expressing health outcomes in terms of QALYs. After the Appendix, I turn to the details of this approach.

APPENDIX: WELFARE ECONOMICS AND PERSON TRADE-OFFS

For simplicity's sake, consider a society that produces two goods X and Y and wonders whether the total production of value could be increased by reallocating resources between these two, in other words, produce less of X and more of Y, or vice versa. To determine this, it needs to compare what economists call the *marginal rate of transformation in production* (MRT) with the *marginal rate of substitution in consumption* (MRS). MRT is the number of additional Ys that could be produced with the resources required to produce the last (marginal) unit of X. For instance, if by producing one unit less of X the society could produce three more units of Y, then MRT is 1X:3Y. MRS, on the other hand, is the number of additional units of Y that would be required to compensate for the loss of value following from the loss of one unit of X. For instance, if total value could be maintained by increasing the consumption of Y by two units if the consumption of X were reduced by one unit, then MRS is 1X:2Y. If the situation in our imaginary society were actually as it is in these numerical examples,

MRT would exceed MRS (1X:3Y versus 1X:2Y). A gain in total value could then be obtained by shifting resources from the production of X to the production of Y. At the margin, reducing the production of X by one unit would allow an increase in the production of Y by 3 units. On the consumption side, an increase of 3 units of Y would more than offset a decrease of 1 unit of X. Hence, there would be a net value gain.

The reader can easily verify for him- or herself that a net value gain would also be obtainable if the marginal rate of transformation were *smaller* than the marginal rate of substitution, for instance, MRT = 1X: 3Y versus MRS = 1X:5Y. Then total value would increase by shifting resources from the production of Y to the production of X.

Only when MRT and MRS are equal will there be nothing to be gained from reallocating resources between these two areas of production. That is the same as saying that *the total value would be at its maximum when MRT = MRS, i.e. when the marginal rate of transformation in production equals the marginal rate of substitution in consumption.*

All this is square one in welfare economics. It can be applied directly to health-care evaluation. Indeed, this is precisely the purpose of cost-effectiveness analysis (CEA) in health care: to detect activities between which marginal rates of transformation and marginal rates of substitution are *not* equal, and between which a reallocation of resources would therefore lead to a gain in the total production of value.

In health care a "good" – like X and Y in the examples above – is a specific kind of improvement in health, or, as I shall call it hereafter, a specific kind of health outcome. Curing a person of a pain problem is an example of a health outcome. Saving a person from dying to leading a life in a wheelchair is another example. The marginal rate of transformation between two outcomes X and Y is the number of additional persons who would be given outcome Y if one person less received outcome X. Thus, in health care the marginal rate of transformation in production is a *person trade-off*. This trade-off is given by the relative costs of treatment: If outcomes X and Y cost US$ 3,000 and 1,000 respectively, then three Ys can be had for one X. So there is a marginal rate of transformation – or a person trade-off on the production side – of 1X:3Y.

The marginal rate of substitution on the consumption side would be the number of additional persons receiving outcome Y that would be required to compensate for the loss of outcome X in one person. Again, this is a person trade-off. Say this person trade-off on the consumption side is 1X:2Y. If the person trade-off on the production side is 1X:3Y, then greater value would be obtained by producing less Xs and more Ys (at the margin).

Thus, just as potential resource allocation improvements in general are detected by comparing marginal rates of transformation and marginal rates of substitution with each other, so potential improvements in resource allocation in health care may in principle be detected by comparing person trade-offs on the production side (= MRT) with person trade-offs on the value side (= MRS).

Chapter 3

QALYs

3.1 WHAT ARE QALYs?

The QALY is a measure of the value of health outcomes. It was developed in the 1960s and early 1970s with a view to resolving the problem of comparing "apples and oranges" in priority setting in health care (Chiang 1965; Torrance 1970; Culyer et al. 1971). The idea was to refer such different outcomes as saved lives, increases in life expectancy, different kinds of functional improvement, and different kinds of symptom relief to the same value scale, whereby it would be possible to compare these various kinds of outcomes with each other.

One of the key features of the QALY approach is the assessment of *the utility of health states*. In economic theory, the concept of utility is defined in different ways. Here I shall be very pragmatic. Broadly speaking, the utility of a health state is the same as the "goodness" of it to the individuals who are in it. By goodness I thus mean the well-being or quality of life associated with the state. (Note that goodness in an ethical sense is not implied.) The goodness of a state can be measured in a number of ways. In the QALY field there are three main techniques. In two of them – the standard gamble and the time trade-off – one measures individuals' willingness to sacrifice life expectancy in order to be relieved of the symptoms and dysfunctions associated with a state. The greater the willingness to sacrifice to become healthy, the lower is the utility – and the greater the disutility – of the health state in question. In the third technique, subjects are asked to locate the health state in question on a rating scale that runs, for instance, from zero to a hundred, where zero may stand for "being dead" and a hundred may stand for "full health." Subjects are instructed to place the state lower on the scale the more undesirable it is.

The utility of health states is expressed on a scale from zero to unity, where zero is the utility of the state "dead" and unity is the utility of the state "healthy." The lower the quality of life associated with a health state, the lower is its utility score on this scale. For instance, being dependent on crutches for walking might score 0.9, while sitting in a wheelchair might score 0.8. Frame 1 explains how utilities are established with the different measurement techniques.

A number of instruments are available for assigning utilities to patients' health states without having recourse directly to the measurement techniques in Frame 1. They are called *multi-attribute utility (MAU) instruments*. Examples are the EuroQol Instrument, the Health Utilities Index, and 15-D (see Table 4 in Section 4.10). They all score individuals on a number of different dimensions of health, such as

---

Frame 1. Techniques for establishing utilities

With the standard gamble technique, the assignment of health-state utilities works as follows. The subject is offered two alternatives. Alternative 1 is a treatment with two possible outcomes: Either the patient is returned to normal health and lives for an additional t years (probability p) or the patient dies immediately (probability 1-p). Alternative 2 has the certain outcome of chronic state i for t years. Probability is varied until the subject is indifferent between the two alternatives, at which point the value for state i is set equal to p.

With the time trade-off technique, two alternatives are offered. One is state i for time t followed by death; the other is healthy for time x. Time x is varied until the respondent is indifferent between the two alternatives, at which point the value for state i is set equal to x/t

With the rating scale technique, values for health states on the scale from zero to unity are obtained simply by asking subjects to locate the states directly on a linear scale. For instance, if a state is located at point 60 on a scale from zero to one hundred, then it receives the value of 0.6.

---

mobility, pain, hearing, and seeing. They then offer a table or a mathematical formula that allows the analyst to transform the multi-attribute health scores – often referred to as "health profiles" – into a single utility number. The transformation algorithms are based on previous research in which one or more of the basic valuation techniques (standard gamble, time trade-off, or the rating scale) were used to establish the utility of different health profiles. I return to a more detailed discussion of the concept of utility and the validity of valuation techniques in Chapter 5.

The QALY approach goes on to make two assumptions about societal values and health benefits. These are:

1. The societal value of a health service is equal to the sum of health benefits that it produces in the persons receiving the service.
2. The health benefit in each individual is the sum of the gains in utility (quality of life) in all the life years in which the individual gets to enjoy the effects of the service.

So if one person gets one additional life year in full health, that is a utility gain of 1 (1–0) for one year, that is, a benefit of $1 \times 1 = 1$ QALY.

If an individual A gets an increase in utility from 0.6 to 0.9 for two years and from 0.6 to 0.7 in the next three years, his/her health benefit is $2 \times 0.3 + 3 \times 0.1 = 0.9$ QALYs. If individuals B and C, by similar calculation, each receives a health benefit of 2.5 and 0.6 QALYs respectively, then the total health benefit for A, B, and C is 4 QALYs (0.9 + 2.5 + 0.6). This is then a numerical estimate of society's valuation of this service for these three individuals. The implication is, for instance, that the service for these three individuals is valued as highly as providing one person with four additional years in full health or four persons with one additional year each in full health.

If a service provides the same utility gain U over the same Y number of years in all the P persons receiving the service, the societal value of the service simply becomes the utility gain (U) times the duration (Y) times the number of persons (P), that is, $U \times Y \times P$ QALYs.

In a more sophisticated version of the QALY model, utility gains are assigned less weight the more distant they are in the future. For instance, a utility gain of 0.5 in Year One of a ten-year life scenario counts as 0.5, while the same gain in the last year of that scenario might count only 0.3. This is called discounting for time preference.

3.2 TWO MAJOR PROBLEMS WITH QALYs

There are many kinds of problems with QALYs, at the ethical, conceptual, and operational levels, see, for example, Froberg and Kane (1989) and Richardson (1991). Here I focus on two major issues.

If we compare the QALY value assumptions with the list shown in Chapter 1 of factors that potentially determine societal value, we see that Factors 1 (number of people), 4 (quality of life), 5 (duration of benefit), and 7 (time preference) are directly covered by the QALY approach. Factor 2 (severity) is indirectly partly covered, inasmuch as, for instance, curing a severely ill person implies a greater improvement in quality of life (Factor 4) than curing a less severely ill person. But the coverage is only partial: For a given increase in quality of life, there is no additional value in the QALY model associated with the severity of the initial condition itself. Similarly, Factor 6 (patient's age) is indirectly partly covered, inasmuch as duration of benefit is strongly correlated with age. Other factors, such as responsibility for own illness (Factor 8), are left out. So a selection of factors has been made. Furthermore, choices have been made with respect to the strength with which each of the factors enters in the value function. According to the model, value is *proportional* both to the number of people receiving help and to the increase they obtain in utility (quality of life), while it is somewhat less than proportional to the duration of the benefit (due to the discounting of future years).

These choices of assumptions were made twenty-five years ago (see, for instance, Culyer et al. 1971). Ideally, one would think that they were made on the basis of empirical studies showing the extent to which societies value different aspects of health-care services. In other words, one would think, or at least hope, that the QALY approach was a result of "reading off" societal values and operationalizing these in a perhaps simplified, but nevertheless mainly realistic, parametric model.

Unfortunately this is not the case. The QALY literature of the early seventies is devoid of empirical data of this kind. The reader will also look in vain for broad, explorative theoretical discussions of the possible determinants of societal value in health care. Instead one finds what I perceive as a quick leap from the way economists tend to think about macroeconomics in general to a simple value judgment within the context of health care: Just as the richness of a country, and hence the goodness of an economy, is measured by the size of its output of goods and services – namely, its GNP – so it is assumed that the goodness of a health care system should be measured in terms of the amount of health that it produces (see, e.g., Weinstein and Stason 1977). From this basic value judgment *in the minds of those who developed the QALY approach* there is only a short step to suggesting that the societal value of a health-care service be viewed as proportional to the increase in quality of life, the duration of benefit (with a discount factor for distance in time), and the number of people helped.

The fact that the QALY model was developed without prior empirical investigation of societal values of course entails a fair risk that the model's basic structure could be flawed. In the next chapter I argue that this is indeed the case. The flaw lies in the assumption that societal value is a simple, unweighted sum of individual health benefits, in other words, that society disregards how a given total amount of benefits is distributed across people. This is referred to as the assumption of *distributive neutrality* (Nord et al. 1995a). While there is increasing recognition among advocates of the QALY approach that this assumption is probably *not quite true* (Williams 1981; Wagstaff 1991; Williams 1994; Garber et al. 1996), there is little realization that it could in fact be *very wrong*. The purpose of Chapter 4 is to marshal evidence showing that the latter is most likely the case.

As we shall see below, QALYs could in principle be assigned *equity weights* to account for distributive concerns (Williams 1988b, Nord et al. 1999). However, there remains another weakness of the QALY approach, namely that the measurement of health benefits in terms of individual utility may not be feasible in the case of health improvements that either are of moderate size or consist in saving peoples' lives. This implies that the QALY approach may in fact not resolve the apples and oranges problem it purports to resolve. I argue this point in Chapter 5.

Together these two weaknesses lead me to propose a different approach to valuing health care in numerical terms, based on asking people to value outcomes not in terms of individual utility to themselves, but rather in terms of appreciation from a broader societal perspective. This is the theme of the final chapter.

Chapter 4

Concerns for Fairness

4.1 WHAT IS FAIRNESS?

In both a caring-for-others and a self-interest perspective, members of society generally feel that some categories of patients have stronger moral claims on scarce health-care resources than others. I shall shortly discuss various factors that determine the strength people assign to such claims. I define a *fair* resource allocation in health care as one that accords with societal feelings about the strength of claims of different patient groups (Broome 1988; Lockwood 1988). A resource allocation that violates such feelings is defined as *unfair*.

4.2 QALYs AND FAIRNESS

The QALY approach rests on the assumption that the health-care system should aim at maximizing health benefits with the resources that are available, irrespective of how these benefits are distributed across people. In the first twenty years of QALYs, this assumption of distributive neutrality was rarely questioned by economists, perhaps because in the field of economics generally it is felt that the role of the economist is to work for efficiency and leave distribution to others. Unfortunately, in the area of health, redistribution is not separable from the achievement of efficiency.

The view of QALYs as ultimate indicators of societal value manifested itself in terms of so called QALY league tables (Williams 1985; O'Kelly and Westaby 1990; Smith 1990). In an often quoted article on "the foundations of cost-effectiveness analysis for health care and medical practices," Weinstein and Stason (1977) recommend that "alternative programs or services are then ranked, from the lowest value to

23

the highest, and selected from the top until available resources are exhausted." Williams (1987a) similarly writes: "The implications of such calculations seems to me to be that we should not expand treatment capacity where cost-per-QALY is high *if* there are untreated patients due to lack of capacity in technologies offering low cost QALYs."

In recent years, there has been increasing recognition that the assumption of distributive neutrality cannot be upheld. Some distributions are viewed as more fair than others; so to maximize the total number of QALYs may be at the expense of fairness. Society may want to strike a balance between producing as many health benefits as possible and treating individuals fairly. Initially these points were made by philosophers and social scientists like Norman Daniels (1985), John Harris (1987), M. Mulkay et al. (1987), D. Brock (1988), John Broome (1988), and Paul Menzel (1990). Gradually the points were taken on board by economists working with the theory of cost-effectiveness analysis (Williams 1988b; Culyer 1989; Loomes and McKenzie 1989; Nord 1989; Mooney and Olsen 1991; Richardson 1991; Wagstaff 1991; Dolan 1988). Perhaps most notable is the recent work of Williams (1997). He argues that a salient ethical basis for rejecting distributive neutrality is the *fair innings argument*, namely, the general sentiment that everyone is entitled to a "normal" lifetime of around 70–75 years, and that anyone failing to achieve this has in some sense been cheated, while anyone getting more than this is living on "borrowed time." Williams addresses the fact that there is a significant difference between social classes in the UK with respect to quality-adjusted life expectancy (QALE) at birth. Adopting a social welfare function of the kind suggested by Wagstaff (1991), Williams gives a hypothetical example of how observations of people's willingness to trade off mean QALE, for equality in QALE could be used to estimate a parameter for the strength of aversion to inequality.

However, in spite of considerable efforts to improve theory, the weight assigned *in practice* to distributive concerns in health economic evaluations remains very small. This has to do with an almost paradoxical attitude demonstrated by those who developed the QALY approach initially and/or later stood behind the development of specific instruments for assigning utilities to health states in concrete cost-effectiveness studies. The attitude has been, on the one hand, to acknowledge that the maximization of health benefits is not the whole story. So estimates of societal value in terms of QALYs should be regarded as only one kind of information that may serve as an aid in resource allocation decisions. On the other hand, there has been very little interest in finding out more precisely in empirical terms how strongly concerns for fairness are felt by the general public and then developing the original QALY model further so as to allow for the encapsulation of these concerns in cost-effectiveness analyses (notable exceptions are Williams 1997 and Dolan 1998). Concern for fairness thus remains an issue to which most analysts in health economics pay tribute only at a ritual level.

An example of this occurs in a book initiated by the United States Department of Health and Human Resources with a view to standardizing the methods of cost-effectiveness analyses in health care (Gold et al. 1996). The book is the product of the deliberations of a panel consisting of some of the foremost academics in the field in North America. The panel's *awareness* of the significance of distributive issues is clear enough:

Even QALYs do not fully reflect what decision makers would like to accomplish in the public interest . . . The simple addition [of QALYs] implies that QALYs are of equal value no matter who gains them or when they occur during their life span. Both intuition and research suggest that this is not the case and that *deviations from the assumption are substantial and important* (Harris, 1987; Daniels, 1993; my italicisation). As a case in point, surveys of the general public (including the elderly) have revealed a strong consensus on the part of the general public, including the elderly, to the effect that the young should be favored over the old (Williams, 1988b; Lewis and Charney, 1989).

The assumption that QALYs are of equal value implies, for example, that it makes no difference whether extra years of healthy life go to people in good health or to people in poor health – perhaps people with a serious disability. Yet decision makers might give preference to those in poor health out of a sense that their need is greater. As another example, a therapy that saved the lives of a few people, allowing them to live many more years in good health, might produce the same number of quality adjusted life years as treating mild arthritis in many people, yet much of the general public would place a higher value on the intervention that helped fewer individuals because it made such a large difference for them. This "aggregation problem" occurs because the numerical sums are equal, but we do not in fact value them equally." (p. 8)

The panel pointed out that "in principle, QALYs received by different people at different times could be weighted before they were added together to reflect the values society places on different circumstances" (p. 8). The idea of such *equity weights* had been introduced earlier by Williams (1988b) and Culyer (1989). However, the panel did not suggest any such weights or indicate criteria on which they might be based. Instead, it limited its discussion to cost-effectiveness analysis in the conventional, utility-oriented sense.

The purpose of the following is to make the magnitude of the discrepancy betweens QALYs and estimates of societal value more apparent. I do so by presenting the totality of evidence that exists today on societal concerns for fairness in health care (for a comprehensive review of the ethical issues, see Menzel et al. 1999). I wish to show that the simple sum of individual valuations of health benefits in terms of QALYs is *not* a largely valid expression of societal value. On the contrary, when we look at public preference data, we find strong reasons to fear that to rank projects in terms of costs-per-QALY as often as not will tend to distort resource allocation decisions rather than inform and aid them.

Concerns for fairness are associated with all the three basic factors of the QALY model – that is, the weight placed on gains in utility, the duration of utility gains, and the number of people helped by health-care programs. Let us look at each of these in turn.

4.3 FAIRNESS AND GAINS IN UTILITY

In particular, there are two aspects of fairness that are emphasized by the general public in evaluating gains in utility and that run counter to the maximization of QALYs. These are illustrated in Figure 2.

Figure 2. *Differences in severity and treatment effect*

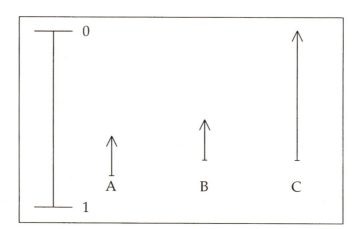

In figure 2, A, B, and C are three groups of patients who on average are alike in all respects except that they have different illnesses. (Note for the argument below that their likeness includes being equal [on average] with respect to preferences for health states). Their health related quality of life (HRQOL) without and with treatment is measured at an interval level of measurement by means of the standard gamble or the time trade-off. A scale from zero to unity is used to express this HRQOL, often referred to as health related utility (hereafter mostly "utility" for short). The bottom end points of the three vertical lines to the right of the scale indicate the utility of patients in the three groups when untreated. The top end points indicate their utility after treatment. (In the following we will, for short, generally refer to the bottom end points as "start points" and the top end points simply as "end points."

Assume that the three groups have the same life expectancy without treatment and that none of the treatments have any effect on life expectancy. Thus the health improvements are pure health-related quality-of-life improvements. Assume also that treatment costs per patient are the same in all three groups.

Given these assumptions, the figure tells us, first, that patients A are *more severely ill* than patients B and C (in the sense that their health-related utility is lower) when no treatment is provided. Second, the figure indicates that the same amount of resources will produce the same benefit – in terms of individually assessed utility – in A and B. Third, while patients in B and C experience the same low level of health-related utility when untreated, a given amount of resources will produce a larger benefit (individual utility gain) in C than in B (the reason being that the groups have different illnesses with different treatability). For short, we may say that group C has a greater potential for health than group B.

If the goal is to maximize QALYs, group C will be given first priority, while A and B will share second place.

There are two concerns for fairness we believe are particularly salient in priority setting in health care that run counter to this rank ordering of groups A, B, and C.

4.3.1 *Severity of Pretreatment Condition*

First, group A is worse off without treatment than groups B and C and may therefore be considered to have a stronger claim to being helped than groups B and C, even if the potential utility gains in the latter groups are equally high (B) or higher (C). Rawls (1971) argued this point forcefully and is supported, for instance, by Callahan (1994): "Our bias, I contend, should be to give priority to persons whose suffering and inability to function in ordinary life is most pronounced, even if the available treatment for them is comparatively less efficacious than for other conditions." In the following we shall for brevity refer to this concern for fairness as the *severity argument*.

Some may argue that the extent to which people have a concern for severity will be captured in their initial *personal* utility assessments of health states. This is only partly true. In utility assessments, for instance by means of the standard gamble or the time trade-off, subjects are not asked about distributive concerns or *societal* value. They are asked to quantify the disutility they personally would feel with different states of illness, and thus – indirectly – to quantify the utility gain they personally would derive from treatment. On the basis of responses to such questions it is possible only to say which of different programs provides the greatest sum of individual utility gains. *The respondents have not expressed any opinion about priority setting*. If one knew that their view on priority setting was that the sum of utility gains should be maximized, then one could *infer* from their utility responses that, for instance in the above example, patients C should have priority over patients A and B. But that doesn't have to be their view. It is perfectly conceivable that a person could think as follows: "I accept that patients in groups A and B seem to value their respective treatments equally much for themselves (in terms of willingness to sacrifice life expectancy). Nonetheless, if I have to make a choice, I would give priority to group A over group B, since they are worse off, and perhaps even over group C, in spite of the greater potential benefit in the latter group." In fact, Callahan shows in the quotation above that he is an example of a person thinking this way. We shall see below that he is far from the only one.

4.3.2 *Realization of Potential for Health*

The other concern for fairness we wish to draw attention to has to do with the comparison between B and C. In terms of QALYs gained, C scores better than B. However, it may be seen as unfair to hold against patients in group B that they happen to have a lesser degree of treatability than group C. Their potential for health improvement is still substantial and important to themselves, and they are just as ill as the patients in group C.

Medical ethicists have addressed an analogous problem – referred to as "the fair chances/best outcomes problem" – in so-called micro-rationing, that is, rationing at the individual level, for instance in the allocation of scarce organs for transplantation (Daniels 1985; Brock 1988; Kamm 1989; Menzel 1990). Assume, for instance, that two people A and B are the same age, have waited in line for the same amount of time, and will each live only one week without a heart transplant. With the transplant, however, A is expected to live two years and B twenty. Who should get the transplant? Daniels (1985) and Harris (1987) discuss a similar problem in "macrorationing": An intervention, A, preserves life in a given group of people and restores these to full health, while another service, B, preserves life in a different group of people but leaves them in a disabled state. All else being equal, should A have priority? In both the microrationing and the macrorationing cases one may ask why those with a lesser outcome should give up their chances of receiving something valuable to them just because somebody else can benefit even more. Harris argues strongly against such discrimination, while Daniels, when reviewing the ethical debate in the literature, concludes that in neither of the above contexts is it clear what would be a fair allocation rule. He reaches this conclusion even after considering arguments invoking people's self-interest behind a veil of ignorance. In a response to Harris, Williams (1987b) seems to concede that the issue has no clear *logical* answer, which leads him to conclude that "at the end of the day, we simply have to stand up and be counted as to which set of principles we wish to have underpin the way the health care system works."

Altogether, though ambiguities exist, ethical reflection seems to suggest that society may not want to discriminate as strongly against those with a lesser potential as pure QALY maximization would suggest. We shall refer to this as the *realization-of-potential argument*.

4.3.3 *Aversion to Inequalities in Health*

There is a third aspect of fairness which needs to be noted here, even if it is beyond the scope of this chapter to examine it in detail. Assume that only one of groups A, B, and C in Figure 2 can be treated, and that group C is given priority over groups A and B. Then inequality in health among the three groups, that is, the differences between the resulting *end states*, will be greater than if group B, or particularly group A, were given priority. Such increased inequality may also be seen as undesirable.

Note that aversion to inequality may occur as an independent concern. While it will necessarily work in the same direction as the realization-of-potential argument, it may both support and run counter to the severity argument, depending on the health outcomes in question. What we above called the severity argument thus refers to the concern for the worst off per se.

Aversion to inequality between end states is not a theme of this chapter, the reason being that it has not been much explored quantitatively. It is, however, certainly an issue for further research.

4.4 WAYS OF MEASURING CONCERNS FOR FAIRNESS

Obviously, the idea of maximizing QALYs will be more misconceived the stronger the concerns for severity and realization-of-potential are felt by society. Two kinds of data may indicate to us how strongly these concerns are felt. First are data expressing in ordinal, verbal terms which criteria society thinks should count most in valuing and prioritizing among health-care services. Second are data expressing the strength of such preferences in cardinal (numerical) terms. The latter kind of data could potentially serve to determine equity weights that could be used to rectify biases in QALY calculations as estimations of societal value.

One possible approach to establishing equity weights is to measure the strength of society's aversion to inequality in health outcomes. Wagstaff (1991) specifies a social welfare function that includes a parameter reflecting the strength of this aversion. In principle, the parameter may be estimated by asking members of a society how much they are willing to sacrifice in the total production of QALYs across individuals or groups of individuals in order to obtain a more even distribution of health among those individuals or groups. Williams (1997) advocates this approach at a theoretical level. It was used by Dolan (1998) in a pilot empirical study (results are reported briefly at the end of this chapter).

Another way to obtain cardinal data on concerns for fairness, which has been used by a number of researchers, exploits the fact that when QALYs count equally much no matter who gets them, utilities have direct implications in terms of person trade-offs. For instance, taking ten people from utility level 0.8 to 1.0 will, in the QALY maximization approach, be just as valuable as taking ten other people from 0.2 to 0.4. The degree to which this implication of utilities accords with actual societal values may be checked by asking representatives of a society to value the two improvements in question directly in terms of person trade-offs. This could, for instance, be framed as follows: Here are two equally costly programs. One will take ten patients from utility level 0.2 to 0.4. The other program will take some other patients from 0.8 to 1.0. *How many patients would the latter program have to include for you to consider the two programs equally worthy of funding?* Now, assume that people on average tend to be indifferent between a program that would help ten persons from 0.2 to 0.4 and a program that would help fifty persons from 0.8 to 1.0. This factor of five then tells us the additional weight that these people wish to assign to QALYs provided to patients with an initial severity level of 0.2 relative to patients with an initial severity level of 0.8.

Alternatively, the concern for severity could be measured by comparing services that cure people at different initial severity levels. Assume, for instance, that one category of patients is at level 0.2 and another at level 0.6. Then curing ten patients in the former category yields the same QALY gain as curing twenty patients in the latter category. Assume, however, that society is indifferent between a program that would cure ten people in the former category and a program that would cure a hundred people in the latter category. Then one would implicitly have observed a fairness-weight in favor of the more severely ill category in the order of a factor of five (100:20).

The concern for treating patients with different potentials for health equally can be measured similarly. Assume, for instance, that two categories of patients are both at level 0.6. One can be helped to 0.8, while the other can be helped to 1.0 (full health). Then helping ten patients in the latter category yields the same QALY gain as helping twenty patients in the former category. Assume, however, that society would be indifferent between a program that would help ten patients in the latter category and a program that would help twelve patients in the former. Then the ratio 12:20 reflects the degree to which society would *discount* the difference in QALYs gained that derives from the difference in the potential for health.

Let us now look at the various data that exist regarding societal concerns for fairness along the various lines mentioned above.

4.5 SOCIETAL CONCERNS FOR SEVERITY

In 1986, a group of health-care politicians, health administrators, health-care personnel, and representatives of patients were commissioned by the Norwegian government to set out guidelines for prioritizing in the Norwegian National Health Service (Norwegian Priority Committee 1987). One of the main conclusions of the committee was that severity of illness should continue to be the most important criterion for prioritizing between patients, although this criterion should be considered together with the effectiveness of treatment. Since then, similar positions have been adopted by government-appointed commissions in several other countries, Holland (Dutch Committee on Choices in Health Care 1992), New Zealand (Campbell and Gillett 1993), and Sweden (Swedish Health Care and Medical Priorities Commission 1993). Studies of population preferences support these official government positions.

In a study among 150 Norwegian politicians involved in health-care decision making at the county level (Nord 1993b), the subjects were presented with the following problem:

Imagine an illness A that gives *severe* health problems and illness B that gives *moderate* problems. Treatment will help patients with illness A *a little*, while it will help patients with illness B *considerably*. The cost of treatment is the same in both cases. There is insufficient treatment capacity for both illnesses, and an increase in funding is suggested. Three different views are then conceivable:

1. Most of the increase should be allocated to treatments for illness B, since the effects of these are greater.
2. Most of the increase should be allocated to treatments for illness A, since these patients are more severely ill.
3. The increase should be divided evenly between the two groups.

Which of these views comes closest to your own?

Only 11 percent placed the main emphasis on the size of the treatment effect (option 1). Thirty-eight percent chose the second option (main emphasis on severity), while 45 percent chose the third view (divide evenly). Note that even this last option represents a rejection of simple QALY maximization.

Ubel (1997) obtained very similar results when he replicated the study in the U.S., using 479 subjects selected for jury duty in Philadelphia (9, 26, and 64 percent for options 1–3 respectively). However, he also found that the responses were sensitive to the wording of the response options. Moreover, when option 3 (equal priority) was omitted as an explicit option, there was only a small majority in favor of giving priority to the more severely ill when Nord's original wording was used. Ubel nonetheless concludes that the study "adds to evidence suggesting that many people place priority on allocating resources to severely ill patients, even when they would benefit less from treatment than others."

In an early empirical person trade-off test of health-state utilities, Nord (1991) compared societal valuations of cures for patients with different degrees of severity of their initial condition. Severity was first judged by having subjects assign utility scores to the various conditions by means of a rating scale. The person trade-offs implied by these ratings were then compared with the person trade-offs that the subjects indicated when asked to make direct comparisons between curative programs for the different patient groups in question. In general, the directly measured person trade-offs in favor of the more severely ill were much higher than the trade-offs implied by the differences in utility produced by the various treatments. To see the strength of the observed preferences for giving priority to the severely ill, consider the following states: (*a*) Unable to work, unable to pursue family and leisure activities, strong pain, depressed; (*b*) Unable to work, moderate pain; (*c*) Moderate pain.

The rating scale values for these states were in the order of 0.20, 0.60 and 0.85, respectively, implying a person trade-off of 1:2 between cures for A and B and roughly 1:5 between A and C. However, in direct person trade-off valuations, restoring one person in state A to full health was typically considered equally valuable as curing 50 people in state B and 100 people in state C.

I later did a series of workshops with health politicians, planners, professionals, and patients in different counties in Norway, as well as in personal interviews with members of the above mentioned Priority Committee (Nord 1993a; Nord 1994b). I described various improvements in health as upward movements on a seven-level disability scale that purported to have approximately equal distances between each of the levels (see Table 13 in Chapter 6). Subjects were asked to compare movements that started at different levels of severity but were equal in size as measured by the number of levels that were gained. There was a clear preference for improvements starting at

Table 1. *Responses to the question "How much more ill are you in state X than in state 'no disability, mild distress'?"*

Distress:	None	Mild	Moderate	Severe
Disability:				
None		1	2	7
Slight social	2	3	5	14
Severe social/				
slight work	4	6	9	18
Severe work	7	9	12	26
Unable to work	11	13	20	60
Confined to				
wheelchair	25	31	64	200
Confined to bed	65	87	200	500

lower levels over equidistant improvements starting at higher levels. For instance, the person trade-off between a movement from level 5 to level 3 and a movement from level 3 to level 1 would typically be in the order of 1:5. Ubel et al. (1998b) later used the same scale to find a preference for emphasizing severity both in curative and preventive programs.

In England, Rosser and Kind (1978) asked a convenience sample of patients, doctors, nurses, and health people to compare various states of illness with a light reference state ("mild distress, no physical disability"). For each state X, the subjects were asked to indicate by a numerical factor "how much more ill a patient in state X is than a patient in the reference state." They were asked to indicate such numbers *with the additional information that the numbers would be interpreted in terms of person trade-offs and as having implications for resource allocation.* The results (medians) were as in Table 1. The numbers may be interpreted as the relative values the subjects would place on cures for patients in the different states. As the reader can see, the values increase very rapidly with increasing severity.

The societal concern for *life saving* was addressed in a joint Norwegian-Australian study (Nord and Richardson et al. 1993). Subjects were asked how they, thinking of themselves as members of parliament, would evaluate two equally expensive proposed special units A and B. Unit A would save ten people per year from dying and restore full health. Unit B would restore to full health a number of people in the following state: "sitting in a wheelchair, pain most of the time, unable to work." The question put to the subjects was: How many patients must be treated in unit B per year in order that you would find it just as valuable to spend the money on unit B as on unit A? The median responses in Norway and Australia were 50 and 40, respectively. In another group of subjects, the condition treated in unit B was described instead as follows: "uses crutches for walking, light pain intermittently, unable to work." The median responses were then 110 and 85.

An exercise similar to the one above was given to members of the Norwegian Priority Commission. In this case, life saving was compared with curing people in the following condition: "severely reduced mobility; can sit, but need help to move about, both at home and outdoors." The person trade-offs expressed by the members of the committee varied from 1 to 1,000. Nine out of eleven chose a number between 10 and 100. The median was 50 (versus 10 lives saved). This fits well with the results of the Norwegian/Australian study.

In Rosser and Kind's study, subjects were asked to add a number for being dead after having provided numbers for all the states in Table 1. The median number for being dead was 200. Again, this may be interpreted as the relative value placed on life saving. The value is three times as high as the value placed, for instance, on curing people confined to a wheelchair and in a state of moderate distress. It is thirty times as high as the value placed on curing people whose "performance at work is very severely limited" due to their illness.

Life saving was also valued very highly in a preference study in a group of Spanish doctors and students (Pinto 1994). For instance, a person trade-off of 1:10 was found between a program that would save a life and a program that would cure people in the following state: "some problems with walking about and washing or dressing, unable to perform usual activities, moderate pain, moderately depressed."

Pinto later found a very similar structure of concern in a group of thirty economics students (Pinto 1997). For instance, one of the states considered was: "some problems with walking about, unable to work, moderately depressed." The standard gamble score obtained for this condition was 0.81, implying that one life saved would be equivalent – in terms of QALYs gained – to curing approximately five people of

Table 2. *Implied and directly measured person trade-offs*

	Implied X	Directly measured X
1 Appendicitis vs X headaches	10	800
1 Appendicitis vs X knee damages	17	12,000
1 Appendicitis vs X cysts	100	No trade-off. Always priority to appendicitis
1 Headache vs X knee damages	1,7	17
1 Knee damage vs X cysts	6	30

the condition. However, three different versions of direct person trade-off questions indicated an equivalence ratio more on the order of 1:20.

In a study in the United States, Ubel et al. (1996) obtained data from 42 students regarding their preferences in terms of person trade-offs for interventions that would cure people in four conditions of differing severity. The conditions were a cyst on the hand that would not disturb functioning but would occasionally cause mild pain; knee damage that would prevent people from exercizing, cause some difficulty when walking, and cause moderate pain one hour daily; constant, often severe headaches that could be decreased with medicines but not be eliminated without reducing the ability to concentrate; and appendicitis (which if untreated will cause death within hours or days). Time trade-off scores for the four conditions were: appendicitis: 0.0; headaches: 0.90; knee problem: 0.94; cyst: 0.99 (standard gamble scores were somewhat lower). Implied and directly measured person trade-offs between cures for these conditions were as in Table 2.

As in the studies by Nord (1991) and Pinto (1997), the directly measured person trade-offs are much higher than what pure utility maximization would suggest, most likely reflecting the very strong weight that subjects place on the severity of the initial condition.

Richardson (1997) asked a sample of 78 economics students in Melbourne, Australia, to compare two equally costly projects, A and B. A would take patients from "confined to bed, moderate discomfort" to a somewhat better state. B would take patients from "moderate pain or discomfort" to a somewhat better state. On a rating scale from 0 to 100, the two movements were described as equally large – from 5 to 20 and from 75 to 90, respectively. Patients in the two projects were also described as being prepared to pay equally much (30,000 Australian dollars) for their respective improvements. Fifty-seven percent gave priority to A; 16 percent to B; and 28 percent nominated equal priority. Median person trade-off between A and B was 1:2 (100 in A was judged equally valuable as 200 in B).

Finally, Dolan (1998) asked a sample of 35 economics undergraduates at the University of Newcastle in the United Kingdom to compare an improvement in utility from 0.2 to 0.4 for one patient with an improvement from 0.4 to X for another patient. Dolan asked: What must X be for you to feel that the two patients should have equal priority when health-care resources are scarce? In other words, what is the trade-off between the severity of the initial condition and the size of the health gain? The median response was 0.8. From this one might infer that the subjects on average assigned a severity weight to utility level 0.2 which was twice that of utility level 0.4.

4.6 RULES OF THUMB CONCERNING SEVERITY

The above evidence is scattered and heterogeneous. Nevertheless, it suggests the order of magnitude by which severity of illness seems to be emphasized by people in a number of industrialized countries. To picture this order of magnitude, consider four classes of outcomes, exemplified as follows:

A. *Saving a person's life* and restoring him/her to a healthy one
B. *Curing a person with a severe problem,* for instance, a person who has to sit in a wheelchair, has pain most of the time, and is unable to work
C. *Curing a person with a considerable problem,* for instance, a person who must use crutches to walk, has light pain intermittently, and is unable to work
D. *Curing a person with a moderate problem,* for instance, a person who has difficulty moving about outdoors and slight discomfort, but is able to do some work and has only minor difficulties at home

(In the following I will use the terms "severe," "considerable," and "moderate" in accordance with these examples.)

From "eyeballing" the above data I submit that in the countries Australia, England, Norway, Spain, and the United States the societal appreciation of outcome A seems to be something like 3–6 times as high as that of class B outcomes, 10–15 times as high as that of class C outcomes, and 50–200 times as high as that of class D outcomes. I emphasize that these numbers pertain to valuations of outcomes in decisions about future treatment capacity. *Quantitative models that purport to be useful for estimating the societal value of health-care activities in these countries, as well as in other countries with similar values, must reflect this structure of concern.*

To do this, health states need to be assigned values in the following order of magnitude in the QALY approach:

Severe problem (cf. outcome class B): 0.65–0.85.
Considerable problem (outcome class C): 0.90–0.94.
Moderate problem (outcome class D): 0.98–0.995.

(For instance, if a state scores 0.98–0.995, then the implication is that the value of curing a person in that state is $1/50 - 1/200$ of the value of saving a person from dying to a life as healthy (0.02–0.005 versus 1.0). I shall refer to this required value structure as one that *compresses health states to the upper end of the scale* (Nord 1993c).

4.7 SOCIETAL CONCERNS FOR REALIZING POTENTIALS FOR HEALTH

The previous section shows a strong societal preference for treating the severely ill before the less severely ill. But what if two groups suffer equally and more can be done for one than for the other? In other words, to what extent does the *size of the health improvements* achieved in different patient groups affect their appreciation by society?

As noted earlier, the QALY approach assumes that the societal value of an intervention is proportional to the size of the health improvement. We may call this a utilitarian view. In contrast to this is the view that it is unfair to hold against patients the fact that they happen to have a lesser potential for good health than others, as long as they also can benefit significantly from treatment (Daniels 1985; Harris 1987; Campbell and Gillett 1993). We may call this an egalitarian view.

The Norwegian Priority Committee (1987) argued that all patients have a right to realize their potential for health. One interpretation of this is that as long as the patient's potential for improvement is realized, the size of the improvement is less important – in other words, the degree of societal appreciation of moderate improvement and large improvement should be the same.

Results from public preference measurements vary on this issue. Patrick et al. (1973) asked graduate students and health leaders in New York City to evaluate in person trade-off terms saving the lives of people in different states of disability in relation to saving the lives of nondisabled people. Priority was clearly given to the latter category. For instance, saving the life of a nondisabled person was considered approximately equivalent to saving the lives of three people in wheelchairs unable to work. One interpretation of this result is that life saving was valued more highly "the more health that was saved," namely, a utilitarian view.

Subsequent events suggest that these results may not be generally valid in the United States today. One of the main reasons for the rejection by the Bush administration of the Oregon prioritization plan in 1992 was that it would discriminate against the permanently disabled and chronically ill, in whom the potential for health tends to be lower than in other people (*Time* [magazine], August 17, 1992).

Data in Norway tend to support the egalitarian rather than the utilitarian view. In a small-scale study using the person trade-off technique, I found that subjects were in general *not* willing to give priority to treating people with a greater potential for benefiting if this meant treating fewer people (Nord 1993d). The egalitarian view was particularly strong in people with an education below the college level. The subjects rationalized their responses by pointing to equality between individuals in value of life and entitlement to treatment irrespective of differences in potential for health. I suggested, though, that there might be a threshold effect here: If the potential for gaining health is only very small in absolute terms, then it is more likely that people will be prepared to discriminate against those with a lesser potential.

In the study mentioned earlier among 150 Norwegian politicians involved in health-care decision making at the county level (Nord 1993b), the subjects were asked the following:

Imagine two illnesses A and B. They are equally common and cause the same degree of suffering. Treatment will help patients with illness A *a little*, while it will help patients with illness B *considerably*. The cost of treatment is the same in both cases. There is insufficient treatment capacity for both illnesses, and an increase in funding is suggested. Two different views are then conceivable:

1. Most of the increase should be allocated to treatments for illness B, since the effects of these are greater.
2. The increase should be divided evenly between the two groups, on the grounds that they suffer equally and are equally entitled to treatment.

Which of these views comes closest to your own?

Seventy-two percent chose the second view (egalitarian), while 24 percent chose the first one (utilitarian). The preference for the egalitarian view was particularly strong in women, older people, those with less than college-level education, and members of parties to the left.

In a survey conducted in Australia (Nord and Richardson et al. 1995), subjects were given a choice between the following options:

1. Among patients who are suffering equally, some priority should be given to those who will be helped most from treatment.
2. Among patients who are suffering equally, those who can become a little better should have the same priority as those who can become much better.

Fifty-three percent chose option 1, while 47 percent chose option 2 (N = 551). There was a slight tendency for the former to find their choice more difficult. The preference for option 2 was stronger in women than in men. It should be noted that option 1 used the expression "some priority," which in itself is an expression of weak preference. On the other hand, option 2 compared those who can become only "a little better" with those who can become "much better." This description of a quite large difference in outcome did not make option 2 an obvious choice. Nonetheless, 47 percent chose option 2. Altogether, the observed distribution suggests that the *size* of the potential health improvement is of moderate importance in Australians' valuations of interventions for different patient groups.

It is well known that societal decision makers may experience psychological burdens when having to make choices about resource allocation (see, e.g., Sen 1997). Pinto and Perpinan (in press) hypothesize that subjects therefore, in studies like the ones referred to above, may have chosen the equal priority option even if they actually felt that the size of the outcome should matter in allocating scarce resources across patients. Pinto and Perpinan tried to overcome this potential bias by conducting a study in two separate groups of subjects (78 and 71 economics students, respectively). In the first group, subjects were told that they had to distribute a certain amount of money between two patients, Juan and Andres. Each million Spanish pesetas invested in Juan would provide an extra year of healthy life, while each extra year of healthy life in Andres would cost *two* million pesetas. The subjects were first asked how they would split the available money between Juan and Andres. Then they were asked how they would split the money if the extra years for Juan were healthy ones, while the extra years for Andres (the more costly of the two) would be years in dialysis. In the second group, subjects were only asked the second question.

With the first question in the first group, where the post-treatment state was full health for both Juan and Andres, 74 percent of the subjects said they would divide the money so as to provide A and B with the same number of additional years. We may call this a strictly egalitarian choice. The percentage was 68 – only slightly lower – in group 1 when the post-treatment state of Andres was changed from full health to "in dialysis." In the second group, however, which looked only at different outcomes for Juan and Andres, as little as 29 percent chose the strictly egalitarian option. The majority preferred a distribution of the available money that would give more life years to Juan than to Andres. However, even 70 percent of this majority would spend at least 40 percent of the available money on Andres, which means that they clearly rejected QALY maximization.

The essential difference between the preference measurement in groups 1 and 2 was that subjects in group 1 were asked directly what consequence it should have that the post-treatment state of Andres was changed from full health to "in dialysis." Pinto and Perpinan suggest that this is too tough a question to put explicitly to people, and that the implicit way of asking, as done in group 2, will elicit truer preferences. However, an alternative interpretation is possible: Subjects in group 1 might, to a greater extent than subjects in group 2, have been stimulated to think about the ethical justification of discriminating against a person with a lesser potential for health, and on the basis of such serious reflection found it unjustified. In this interpretation, the responses in group 2 may be seen as a result of lack of reflection rather than as showing "true" preferences.

The Spanish study also contains the difficulty that concerns for the size of the health benefit may have interacted with concerns for the cost differential between the two patients (one being twice as expensive to treat as the other). It seems reasonable that people may prefer to treat a low-cost patient with a large potential for improvement (Juan) before a high-cost patient with a low potential for improvement (Andres, in question 2). From this it does not follow, however, that people find it ethical to discriminate on the basis of differences in potential only.

Pinto and Perpinan conclude that people, when thinking about priority setting, *are* concerned about the size of the health benefit that different patients can obtain, but not as strongly as is assumed in the QALY maximization approach. With this general conclusion I agree.

In summary, I submit that, in valuing interventions for different patient groups, the degree to which people emphasize the size of the treatment effect varies. It does seem clear, however, that in a country like Norway the societal valuation of health outcomes is much less tightly related to their *size* than what is suggested in conventional health economics theory. People tend to feel that equally ill people have (or should have) much the same right to treatment irrespective of whether the treatment effect is large or moderate. This view seems to be shared by a considerable portion of the Australian population and is not incompatible with data from a Spanish convenience sample. It has also been expressed strongly in bioethical debate in England, New Zealand, Sweden, and the United States.

4.8 RULES OF THUMB CONCERNING SEVERITY AND POTENTIALS FOR HEALTH

The rules of thumb formulated earlier concerning severity encapsulate to some degree egalitarian views regarding potentials for health. Consider four planned services, A, B, C, and D, for patients in life-threatening conditions. A will restore the patients to full health, whereas B, C, and D will leave the patients with moderate, considerable, and severe problems respectively. With health-state values as in the rules of thumb, there will be small differences between the valuations of services A, B, and C (1.0, 0.98–0.995, and 0.90–0.94), and even the outcomes of service D will score 0.65–0.85 of the outcomes of service A. Similarly, the value of helping patients with severe or considerable problems will vary only moderately with the degree to which they are helped.

We may therefore regard the value structure suggested in the rules of thumb as encapsulating, not only societal concerns for severity, but also to a reasonable degree concerns for fairness between patient groups with different potentials for benefiting from treatment. *Quantitative models that purport to be useful for estimating the societal value of health-care activities, must – at least roughly – reflect this structure of concern.*

4.9 THE SELF-INTEREST PERSPECTIVE BEHIND A VEIL OF IGNORANCE

The rejection of health benefit maximization that is suggested by the above data refers to resource allocation in a *caring-for-others perspective.* Some will argue that such rejection would be foolish in a perspective of long-term self-interest behind a veil of ignorance, and consequently that, if these same questions had been framed in such a perspective, the responses would have been different. What does the evidence tell us about this? Unfortunately the evidence is very limited. However, four studies give us some indication.

In the workshops mentioned earlier with health politicians, planners, professionals, and patients in different counties in Norway (Nord 1994b), subjects were asked to compare various pairs of projects, where in each pair the patients' initial functional levels were the same while the level resulting from treatment was higher in one project than in the other. The subjects were placed in the role of health planners. That is, they were asked to distribute resources between groups of other people. Given this role, they generally expressed some degree of willingness to give priority to those who would benefit more. However, it was hypothesized that the subjects might take a different view if they were to choose between different sets of rules for prioritizing that could have consequences for themselves as potential future patients. They were therefore also presented with the following problem: Assuming that you do not know what kind of illnesses you yourself might contract in the future, which of two hospitals A and B would you rather belong to, one that gives equal priority to patients with equal initial severity of illness as long as the treatment effect is substantial in either case (hospital A) or one that gives priority to those with a greater potential for improvement (hospital B). As the reader can see, the question placed the subjects behind a veil of ignorance and therefore, in a sense, elicited unbiased preferences. The results are shown in Table 3.

Table 3. *Preferences for admission rules behind a veil of ignorance*

Hospital:	A	B
Rule:	Equal priority even if out- comes differ	Priority to better outcomes
Preferred by (number of subjects):	31	20

Out of 51 subjects, 31 preferred to belong to hospital A (equal priority), while 20 preferred to belong to hospital B (priority to better outcome). *This means that a majority of those who gave priority to the better-outcome option in the role of health planners did not themselves wish to go to a hospital that followed such a practice.* In ensuing discussions it appeared that most people believed that their evaluation of receiving treatment would be determined primarily by how ill they were and not so much by *how much* they could be helped, as long as the help would be substantial.

A similar pattern of responses was observed in a second study involving personal interviews with members of the Norwegian Priority Committee (Nord 1994b).

A third study was conducted in Australia (Richardson and Nord 1997). A group of 83 people living in Melbourne who had earlier participated in a national survey of health issues were recruited for personal interviews. They were randomized to two different kinds of person trade-off questions. Half the group were asked to think of themselves as planners assigned the task of deciding which of two different life-saving projects should receive funding. One was expected to save the lives of ten people and restore them to a given state of disability that was described in some detail. The other would allow a smaller number of lives to be saved, but the patients would be restored to full health. The subjects were asked to indicate the number of lives saved in the latter case that would make them regard the two projects as equally attractive. This, in other words, was a person trade-off question asked in a caring-for-others perspective. It was asked twice, using two different states of disability as end states in option 1.

The states of disability, called A and B below, had previously received time trade-off scores of 0.75 and 0.55 respectively.

The other half of the subjects were asked to consider options with precisely the same outcomes as those described above (life saving to healthy versus to states A and B, respectively), however in a more personalized context. First, they were asked to consider two long-term units rather than two short-term projects, and second, they were asked "not to think of yourself as a planner or administrator, instead . . . have in mind the interests of the patients concerned, including your own interests as someone who might be needing one of these units one day." The subjects were told that their own chance of getting either of the illnesses in question was the same, about 1 in 100. This, in other words, was a person trade-off question asked in a self-interest perspective behind a veil of ignorance.

In the caring-for-others (CFO) perspective, 6–7 lives restored to full health were considered as valuable as 10 lives restored to state A. In the self-interest (SI) perpective, this ratio was 9.5 to 10. In other words, *less* emphasis was placed on the difference in the size of the health benefit to each individual in the self-interest perspective than in the caring-for-others perspective. The same was found when state B was used as the disability end state. Here the ratios were 3–4 to 10 in the CFO perspective, compared to 5–6 to 10 in the SI perspective. With both disability states, the differences across perspectives were statistically significant.

As noted earlier, Ubel (1997) replicated the study by Nord (1993b) about the importance of severity. Some of his respondents were given a modified set of response options:

Imagine an illness A that gives *severe* health problems and illness B that gives *moderate* problems. Treatment will help patients with illness A *a little*, while it will help patients with illness B *considerably*. The cost of treatment is the same in both cases. There is insufficient treatment capacity for both illnesses, and an increase in funding is suggested. Three different views are then conceivable:

1. Most of the increase should be allocated to treatments for illness B, involving moderate health problems which improve considerably with treatment.
2. Most of the increase should be allocated to treatments for illness A, involving severe health problems which improve a little with treatment.
3. The increase should be divided evenly between the two groups.

Which of these views comes closest to your own?

This version, which is about caring for others, was presented to 77 subjects. Seventy-eight other subjects were asked precisely the same question, however in a self-interest perspective behind a veil of ignorance: "In making your policy recommendation, consider the possibility that you will be a patient affected by this policy and that you have an equal chance of developing either illness A or illness B." Response distributions on options 1, 2, and 3 respectiveley were 22, 5, and 73 percent in the caring-for-others perspective, versus 14 percent, 10, and 76 percent in the self-interest perspective. That is, there was a slight tendency toward a stronger concern for severity in the self-interest perspective than in the caring-for-others perspective.

The findings in the Australian and American studies are consistent with the observations in the Norwegian ones. In all four studies, the concern for maximizing health benefits seems to be even less in the self-interest perspective than in the caring-for-others perspective. This may seem somewhat puzzling. It is one thing to find that rejection of health benefit maximization occurs not only in the caring-for-others perspective but also in the self-interest perspective; it is another to find that the rejection is even stronger in the latter perspective. However, one possible explanation is this: In what I call the caring-for-others perspective, subjects may be concerned about more than fairness. Placed in a planner's role, they may also be drawn toward a form of businesslike thinking in which the maximization of output for a given amount of resources is the conventional concern. In the self-interest perspective, this businesslike thinking may be replaced by the concern that emerged in the explanation of the responses of the subjects in the Norwegian study, namely, that their evaluation of receiving treatment would be determined primarily by how ill they were and not so much by *how much* they could be helped, as long as the help would be substantial.

It would be incorrect to draw strong conclusions on the basis of these few studies. The samples are small and the methodological pitfalls many. However, it is fair to say that the little evidence that exists does not support the hypothesis that people are health benefit maximizers when thinking about their own long-term self-interests behind a veil of ignorance of their own future needs. The pure counting of votes for different options does not suggest such a preference structure, and the subjects' explanations of their votes indicate an underlying way of thinking that cannot easily be discarded as "irrational."

In the previous section I showed that the assumption of health benefit maximization in the QALY approach is clearly unjustified in the caring-for-others perspective. My conclusion from the present section is that the assumption is also highly questionable in the self-interest perspective.

4.10 THE DEGREE OF ERROR IN UTILITY-BASED PREDICTIONS OF SOCIETAL PREFERENCES

Having established what some Western societies' structure of concern for severity and realization of potentials for health roughly looks like, let us return to the question raised earlier: *How big a mistake does one make if one uses the sum of health benefits in terms of individual utility gains as an estimate of the societal value of a health-care program?*

When answering this question we need to distinguish between utilities as they ideally should be measured, and utilities as they conventionally are estimated in the QALY field. In Chapter 5 I shall argue that there is a difference between these two. At this stage I shall focus on the utilities that health states de facto are assigned in contemporary QALY calculations.

To obtain a broad picture of the latter, a study was undertaken in 1996 of the different multi-attribute utility (MAU) instruments that were available for assigning utilities to health states (Nord 1996a). Main features of the instruments are given in Table 4. All eight instruments have a multidimensional, descriptive system by which any state of illness can be categorized. The number of dimensions ranges from 2 to 15. With some instruments, different dimensions have been valued separately, and additive or multiplicative formulas are applied for calculating values for composite states. With other instruments, composite states have been valued directly and are presented in tables. Valuation techniques vary and include the standard gamble, the time trade-off, and different kinds of ratings scales. Each of the states described in the rules of thumb (severe, considerable, and moderate problems) was scored using each of the eight instruments. Some of the scores were taken from the literature. Others were obtained ad hoc by having two independent judges (a medical doctor and myself) apply the various instruments to the states in question (scores in the literature are based on a similar approach). In a few cases where there was a substantial disagreement between the two judges, we discussed the cases and reached a closer agreement.

Table 4. *Multi-attribute utility instruments*

Name	Dimensions	Valuation technique
The Quality of Well-Being Scale	Mobility, social act, physical act, 25 symptoms	Rating scale on single dimensions; additive formula
The Health Utilities Index Mark I	Physical function, role function, social-emotional, health problem	Rating scale on single dimensions, time trade-off on composite states; multiplicative formula
The Health Utilities Index Mark II	Sensory, mobility, emotion, cognitive, self-care, pain, fertility	Rating scale on single dimensions, rating scale and standard gamble on composite states; multiplicative formula
The EuroQol Instrument	Mobilty, self-care, usual activity, pain, anxiety/depression	Rating scale on composite states
The York EuroQol Time Trade-off Tariff	Same	Time trade-off on composite states
The Index of Health-Related Quality of Life (simple)	Disability, physical discomfort, emotional distress	Standard gamble on composite states
The Index of Health-Related Quality of Life (complex)	Dependency, disharmony, dysfunction, pain/discomfort, symptoms, dysphoria, fulfillment	Multistep rating scale procedure; additive formula
The 15 D	Mobility, vision, hearing, breathing, sleeping, eating, speech, bladder and bowel function, usual activites, mental discomfort, depression, distress, vitality, sexual activity	Multistep rating scale procedure; additive formula
The Rosser-Kind Index	Disability, pain/distress	Magnitude estimation on composite states

The results are summarized in Table 5. They suggest that *none of the eight instruments has sufficient upper-end compression to capture the strength of societal preferences for treating the severely ill before the less severely ill*. In five instruments, the bias is so strong that the instruments are completely unusable, at least as stand-alone aids, in comparisons of treatment programs for patient groups that differ with respective to the severity of their condition (the QWB, HUIM1, HUIM2, and the two EuroQol models). Two instruments (IHQL-complex and the 15-D) assign adequate values to curing people with severe problems relative to life-saving interventions but overestimate society's appreciation of cures for moderate conditions relative to cures for severe ones.

An example will show what these biases could mean in practice. If we use the middle numbers in each interval in Table 5 (e.g., 0.75 in the interval 0.65–0.85), according to the Rules of Thumb the value of curing a person with a severe condition is about 25 times that of curing a person with a moderate condition (1.0–0.75 = 0.25 vs 1.0–0.99 = 0.01). The greater value of curing the severely ill would therefore justify that the cost per intervention for these patients was up to 25 *times as high* as the cost of curing the moderately ill. According to the QWB, however, the cures for the severely ill would be deemed less cost-effective than cures for the moderately ill only if they were more than 2.5 times as costly (1.0–0.50 = 0.50 vs 1.0–0.80 = 0.20). Similarly, with the 15D, the EuroQol TTO, and the HUIM2, the critical cost ratios would be 3, 4, and 7.5 respectively, which is slightly better, but still far from the true societal willingness to accept high cost in treating the severely ill.

In addition to the eight MAU instruments included in the above review, at least three more instruments are presently available: The Health Utilities Index, Mark III (HUIM3: Feeny et al. 1995), the Quality of Life and Health Questionnaire (QLHQ: Hadorn 1995), and the Australian Quality of Life (AQOL: Hawthorne and Richardson 1996). Preliminary data suggest that the HUIM3 produces utilities comparable to those of the HUIM2 (David Feeny, oral presentation at the ISOQOL conference in Vienna, November 1997). Utilities from the two other instruments are not judged here.

The question raised in this section was: Can society's valuation of different health programs relative to each other be estimated by calculating the sum of utility gains that each of the programs provide? I submit that it cannot. But I must stress that the answer pertains to

Table 5. *Health-state scores according to Rules of Thumb and different multi-attribute utility instruments*

	Problem level		
Instrument	Severe	Considerable	Moderate
Rules of thumb	.65–.85	.90–.94	.98–.995
QWB	.45–.55	.65–.70	<.80
HUIM1	.10–.20	.30–.40	<.85
HIUM2	.40	.70	.90–.94
EuroQol	.20	.60	.70
York EuroQol (TTO)	.20–.25	.40–.50	.80
IHQL (3D)	.50–.70	.75–.85	.89–.93
IHQL (complex)	.70–.75	.80–.90	.90–.94
15 D	.77	.86	.91–.93
Rosser-Kind	.68	.94	.97–.98

utilities as they are conventionally estimated, for instance, by means of existing MAU instruments. In the next chapter I shall argue that these estimates are biased. They are based on asking people to value health states that they are not in themselves ("hypothetical" or "imagined" health states), rather than on asking patients to value their own health state. If the latter approach were used, utilities would tend to have stronger upper-end compression, in which case the discrepancy between utilities and health-state scores obeying the Rules of Thumb would be smaller.

4.11 THE IMPORTANCE OF THE DURATION OF A TREATMENT EFFECT

In the basic version of the QALY approach, the societal value of an improvement in health is proportional to the number of years that the recipient gets to enjoy it. For instance, a cure of a given condition will carry twice as much value for a sixty-year-old person with a life expectancy of twenty years as for an equally old person with a life expectancy of only ten years.

The assumption of proportionality between duration and value was adopted in the basic QALY approach without any empirical basis. It was simply the result of the intuition of the constructors of the approach that the societal value of an intervention is higher the greater the amount of well life it produces (see, e.g., Culyer et al. 1971).

The data presented in the previous section supporting the realization-of-potential argument cast doubt on this feature of the QALY approach as well, since a person's life expectancy may be seen as an aspect of his or her potential for benefiting from a treatment. Analogously to the argument presented with respect to quality-of-life improvements for groups B and C in Figure 2, one could argue that it is not fair to hold against patients in one group the fact that they happen to have a shorter life expectancy than patients in another group. Arguably, the remaining life time of people in the former group is as important to them as the remaining life time of people in the latter group.

It is only quite recently that the emphasis society wishes to place on duration of effect has been studied empirically. Olsen (1994) did a pioneer survey in a sample of undergraduate students and medical doctors in Norway. When framing questions in a caring-for-others perspective, he found that ten years of benefit gained by 100 people was considered equivalent in societal value to twenty years of benefit received by 80 people. In other words, 1,000 life years gained in the first case was considered equivalent to 1,600 life years gained in the second case. Or, to put it yet another way, doubling the duration was offset by reducing the number of people treated by only 20 percent (rather than 50 percent). Assuming that societal value is proportional to the number of people treated – as the QALY approach does – this suggests that increasing duration by 100 percent from a starting point of ten years leads to an increase in societal value of 25 percent. This, of course, is far below proportionality.

In a later study, Nord and Richardson et al. (1996) interviewed 42 subjects in Melbourne, Australia, who had earlier participated in a national survey of health issues. The main context described to them was one implying that they themselves could be affected one day by the prioritizing principle for which they opted. More specifically, subjects were asked to consider proposals to establish two highly specialized hospital units. They were told that there were sufficient resources for only one of these. Subjects were presented with eight scenarios. In each of these the money spent on unit A would allow more people to receive treatment, while the alternative unit B promised a lesser number of people the same benefit but for a greater number of years.

Subjects were asked to assume that they themselves had a 1 in 100 chance of contracting either illness.

In the first paired comparison, unit A would save the life of ten people per year and allow them to live in normal health for one year, after which they would die. With unit B, X patients would be saved per year and allowed to live in normal health for five years, after which they would die. An indifference point (X < 10) was established with the aid of a slide board. There were three other paired comparisons of life-extending units, with life expectancies of the patients concerned being five versus ten years, ten versus twenty years and twenty versus thirty years, respectively. There were four similar paired comparisons of units providing health improvements rather than life extension. The patients were described as being "partly bedridden and in slight pain," with the possibility of being restored to full health for the same lengths of time as in the life-extending cases (1 vs. 5, 5 vs. 10, 10 vs. 20, 20 vs. 30 years).

An effort was made to ensure reflective responses by presenting the subjects with arguments in favor of either project. In the life-saving case, the arguments were as follows:

You could argue that people have an equally strong desire for treatment whichever of the two illnesses they happen to get. You might therefore prefer unit A, since this would treat more people and give you a better chance of benefiting one day.

On the other hand, you could argue that it would be more important for yourself and others to have a chance of treatment if it resulted in *five* extra life years rather than *one*. You might for this reason prefer unit B even though it would treat fewer patients. (Italized numbers depended on the specific question being asked.)

Similar arguments were presented in the cases relating to health improvement.

Tables 6 and 7 show that the valuation of benefits was a positive function of duration, as treating fewer people with a longer life expectancy was regarded as equally valuable as treating more people with a shorter life expectancy. However, valuations increased less than proportionately with duration. For example, the first line in Table 6 indicates that 10 (10 × 1) life years provided by unit A were considered equivalent to 17.5 (5 × 3.5) secured by unit B. In Table 8 this result is expressed as a ratio in which each life year gained at unit B on average is worth 0.57 (10/17.5) of the life year gained at unit A

Table 6. *Life-extending interventions (including self-interest)*

Years extended		Equivalent numbers of people helped			
Group A	Group B	A		B (median)	IQR (B)
1	5	10	=	3.5	1.5–6.6
5	10	10	=	6.5	5.0–9.1
10	20	10	=	7.0	5.5–9.0
20	30	10	=	8.5	7.5–9.5

Table 7. *Health-improving interventions (including self-interest)*

Years enhanced		Equivalent numbers of people helped			
Group A	Group B	A		B (median)	IQR (B)
1	5	10	=	2.5	1.5–6.0
5	10	10	=	6.8	4.9–9.1
10	20	10	=	6.5	5.5–9.0
20	30	10	=	7.5	6.4–9.1

Table 8. *Ratios derived from Tables 6 and 7*

Comparison		Life-saving	Health-improving
Unit A	Unit B	*Life years A/B*	*Life years A/B*
1	5	0.57	0.80
5	10	0.77	0.74
10	20	0.71	0.77
20	30	0.78	0.89

(column 3). The other results shown in Table 8 may be interpreted correspondingly. In all cases, there is a marked discounting of additional life years gained in unit B, both in the context of life extending and health improvement.

As noted above, these results were obtained from questions framed in a self-interest perspective behind a veil of ignorance. One group of subjects was also asked to compare programs with 10 and 20 years duration in a caring-for-others perspective (imagining themselves as members of a State Health Board). Somewhat *greater* emphasis seemed to be placed on the duration of benefit in that perspective (5.5 persons × 20 years = 10 persons × 10 years both in the life-extending and the health-improving case).

In sum, the studies by Olsen and by Nord and Richardson et al. provide support to the assumption in the QALY approach that the societal value of an outcome is a positive function of the number of years that recipient gets to enjoy it. At the same time, the studies suggest that to assume that societal value is *proportional* to duration is going too far. This seems to apply to both the caring-for-others and the self-interest perspectives.

These findings are supported by a recent study in England in which views on the importance of duration were elicited in a series of six focus groups. Subjects seemed to emphasize differences in duration only when duration was short. For instance, they would value a four-year effect clearly higher than a two-year effect, but at the same time not discriminate strongly between a ten-year effect and a twenty-year effect (Dolan and Cookson 1998). Chris Murray argues along the same lines when reporting on a preference study among 69 students from various countries at the Harvard School of Public Health (see Murray and Lopez 1996, p. 62). The argument is consistent with the threshold effect that was hypothesized earlier regarding subjects' willingness to discriminate against people with a lesser potential for improvements in functioning and quality of life: As long as an obtainable health gain is substantial to the individual concerned, it should not be held against him or her that other individuals might obtain even greater gains from the same resources.

The willingness to discriminate between patients with different capacities to benefit nonetheless seems to be stronger when benefit is measured in terms of duration, as in the studies by Olsen (1994) and Nord and Richardson et al. (1996), than when benefit is measured in terms of improvements in quality of life (compare the studies by Nord 1993b; Nord 1993d; and Nord and Richardson et al. 1995, referred to earlier). An explanation offered by Singer et al. (1995) could be that quality of life is difficult to measure. Many people may feel that they have no right to pass judgment on how good or bad different states of illness will be for other people. In fact, this was explicitly stated by several subjects in the study by Nord (1993d). With differences in duration, on the other hand, there is no such problem of judgment; hence people may also feel that there is a more legitimate basis for discriminating among different patient groups.

However, it must be stressed that the number of subjects in the studies referred to above was extremely small. It is also possible that the results on duration are in part artifacts of the person trade-off technique. Particularly when a slide board is used as a visual aid, it is conceivable that the technique encourages people to engage in numerical trade-offs rather than to keep in mind principles of equal entitlement to treatment (Nord and Richardson et al. 1996). The empirical basis – in terms of public preference data – for judging the relationship between duration and societal value therefore remains unsatisfactory.

4.12 DOES DISCOUNTING FOR TIME PREFERENCE SOLVE THE DURATION PROBLEM?

In principle, if society is concerned about people's right to realize their potential for health, and therefore assigns values to given health improvements as a less-than-proportional function of life expectancy, then this may be incorporated into QALY calculations by assigning marginally decreasing value to health gains provided to an individual over a series of life years. For example, if a given health gain corresponds to a value of say, 0.5 on the 0–1 utility scale, then the total value of the gain over a series of years could be counted as a sum of 0.5 in the first year and then, for instance 0.4 in the second year, 0.3 in the third year, and so on.

Such discounting of values in future years is standard practice in QALY calculations. One may therefore argue that a possible societal concern for allowing people to realize their potential for health whatever their life expectancy is, and hence for not discriminating against people with a lower life expectancy, is in fact already incorporated into the QALY approach.

This is to some extent true. But there are two reasons to doubt that the discounting of future values being practiced in the QALY approach correctly represents societal preferences for discounting duration.

The first reason is at the analytical level. The original purpose of discounting for time in the QALY approach was to honor the fact that society tends to value an outcome less the later it occurs. Consider, for instance, three interventions for patients A, B and C that have identical effects of, say, twenty years' duration but are performed at three different points in time, namely one week, two years, and ten years from now, respectively. In the QALY approach, the outcome occurring in ten years is assumed to be valued less by society than the identical outcome occurring in two years, and even less than the one that occurs in the immediate future. To capture this, each of the outcomes is discounted to their so-called present value at some annual rate.

The important thing to note here is that the purpose of this discounting is not to reduce the value of each twenty-year scenario to something less than twenty times the value of a one-year scenario (which would be to discount for duration). Rather, the purpose is to discount for the scenarios' distance in time. To see the difference clearly, assume, for example, an annual discount rate of 3 percent, as presently recommended in North America (Gold et al. 1996). Discounting for a scenario's distance in time should then be done by dividing the value of the twenty-year-long scenario by 1.03^{10} in the case of patient C and by 1.03^2 in the case of patient B, while no discounting would be required in the case of patient A. However, in standard QALY calculations, it is not whole scenarios that are discounted in one single operation. Instead, each life year in a scenario is viewed as an independent event, the value of which is discounted according to its specific distance in time. The scenario of patient A will then be assigned a value equal to the value of the first year, plus the value of the second year divided by 1.03, plus the value of the third year divided by 1.03^2 and so on. This effectively amounts to discounting duration, inasmuch as the total value of scenario A will be less than the value of the first year multiplied by twenty. But the *rate* of discounting (3 percent) derives from time preference data, not from data on societal views on the importance of duration. So it would only be random if the discount rate used in QALY calculations actually corresponded with the strength of societal preferences for treating people with different life expectancy equally.

The other point is judgmental. A discount rate of 3 percent means that ten life years starting now have a present value of 8.5, while twenty years starting now have a present value of 14.5. A 3 percent discount rate, in other words, means that increasing duration by 100 percent from a starting point of ten years leads to an increase in societal value of 70 percent (from 8.5 to 14.5). This is much higher than what is indicated by the little empirical evidence that exists (see the studies by Olsen, Nord and Richardson et al., and Dolan). Intuitively it also seems high given the limited emphasis that society wishes to place on differences in the size of outcomes in analogous circumstances, namely, when people have different potentials for improvements in functioning and quality of life.

I conclude that the way in which the duration of benefits is valued in the QALY approach initially had no empirical basis. Later studies of societal preferences for duration are so limited that numerical estimates of the strength of these preferences necessarily will have extremely wide margins of error. However, even if at present it is impossible to estimate the strength of these preferences with any reasonable degree of accuracy, it seems likely that the QALY approach assigns too much value to duration. The discount rate recommended for time preference in contemporary QALY calculations is probably insufficient to encapsulate societal aversion to discriminating between people who are in equal need but have different life expectancies.

4.13 THE IMPORTANCE OF AGE

Because of its emphasis on the number of years people get to enjoy the effect of an intervention, the QALY approach tends to assign greater value to interventions for young people than to interventions for older people. For example, assuming a discount rate of 3 percent per year, curing a sixty-year-old of a given condition will be assigned 70 percent more value than curing a seventy-year-old of the same condition, since the former has (roughly) twice the life expectancy of the latter. According to the previous section, such a strong discrimination among age groups on the ground of difference in duration of effect is probably in conflict with societal concerns for allowing people to realize their potential for health whatever their life expectancy is. Indeed, this is why the QALY approach has been called "ageist" (Harris 1987).

However, society may value treating the young more highly than treating the elderly for different reasons than the difference in life expectancy. First, people may feel that, all else being equal, an individual has a greater right to enjoy additional life years the fewer life years he or she has already had. In other words, people may have a preference for equity between patients with respect to total life outcome. This is often referred to as the *fair innings* argument (Harris 1987; Williams 1997). It has also been called *egalitarian ageism*, as opposed to *utilitarian ageism*, which is based on the duration of effect rationale (Nord and Richardson et al. 1996). Second, people may feel that certain stages of an individual's life are socially more important than others (Williams 1988b), for instance, those stages during which they care for their children.

There is, then, the possibility that, while the strength with which the QALY approach favors the young over the elderly cannot be justified on the ground of differences in life expectancy alone, it could be justified if arguments concerning age per se were also taken into account.

To this it must first be added that the QALY approach was not constructed with a view to encapsulating the argument concerning age per se. So if the strength of discrimination between the young and the elderly inherent in the QALY model turns out to be (roughly) correct when both the duration argument and age-per-se arguments are taken into account, then it is because one error in the valuation model (the exaggerated emphasis on duration) is compensated for by another error (the omission of the age-per-se arguments).

But this is a minor point. The proof of a pudding lies not in the cooking but in the eating. The important question is really whether the implications of the QALY model for resource allocation across age groups fit with observed societal preferences. As an example consider an intervention for twenty-year-olds (I-20) with a given degree of discomfort versus interventions I-60 and I-70 for sixty-year-olds and seventy-year-olds, respectively, with the same discomfort. Assuming the same effect of treatment, a QALY model with a 3 percent discount rate will assign values to the three interventions roughly as follows: I-20 is 1.8 times as valuable as I-60 and 3.1 times as valuable as I-70. I-60 is 1.7 times as valuable as I-70. This implies that treating 33 twenty-year-olds will be valued as highly as treating 60 sixty-year-olds and 100 seventy-year-olds. Is this how society actually feels?

The existing evidence does not give a clear answer (for a review, see Tsuchiya 1997). First, most of the evidence is in terms of statements of ordinal preferences for one age group over another rather than in numerical (cardinal) person trade-off terms. Second, unlike what some observers (Williams 1997; Gold et al. 1996) seem to think, the ordinal evidence goes both ways: Studies in Wales, Sweden, Holland, and Japan have shown support for according priority to children and young adults over elderly people (Charny et al, 1989; Bråkenhielm, 1990; Björk and Rosen 1993; Busschbach et al. 1993; Tamura et al. 1995), while studies in Norway and Australia have not (Nord 1993b; Nord and Richardson et al. 1995).

Two studies have used time trade-off questions to find the relative value that people assign to life years at different stages in their own lives. In Holland, Busschbach et al. (1993) found the following implied relative values for ages 5, 10, 35, 60, and 70, respectively: 1.7, 1.6, 1.0, 0.7, 0.7. In Japan, Tsuchiya (1996) found much the same valuation in a sample of young respondents, while the values in a sample of older respondents were 0.6, 0.8, 1.0, 0.5, 0.3. Although both these studies clearly suggest support for policies that favor the young over the elderly, they do not tell us how strong this support is, since it does not follow from *time trade-off* based responses referring to subjects' own lives what *person trade-offs* these subjects would favor in allocating resources across age groups.

Cropper et al. (1994) used person trade-off type questions to establish the value of life-saving programs concentrating on different age groups. They found that saving the lives of people at ages 20, 30, 40, and 60 were valued in ratios of roughly 0.7, 1.0, 0.6, and 0.1, respectively. Similarly, Johannesson and Johansson (1996) found weights of 1.0, 0.16, and 0.05 for ages 30, 50, and 70, assuming 5 percent discounting. Neither of these studies controlled for differences in life expectancy. The results therefore reflect the combined effect of age per se and duration of effect. It is not possible from these data to disentangle the two effects and estimate the effect of age per se.

A study done in Australia by Nord and Richardson et al. (1996) is to my knowledge the only one that allows this. Forty-four subjects recruited from a random population sample in Melbourne were asked to imagine that they were members of a State Health Board. They were asked to choose between equally costly projects that differed with respect to the age and number of patients involved and to express a trade-off between these two factors. *Life expectancy after treatment was described as being the same in all projects (ten years).* For example, the following scenario was presented:

PROJECT A: Imagine an illness A from which patients die within a few months if they are not treated. The patients are typically around *20 years old*. Treatment will enable the patients to continue to live in normal health for 10 years, after which they die. A project is proposed that will allow treating an additional 10 patients with illness A in the next year.

PROJECT B: Now, imagine another illness B from which patients also die within a few months if not treated. The patients are typically around *10 years old*.

Treatment will enable the patients to continue to live in normal health for 10 years, after which they die. A project is proposed that will allow treating an additional x patients with illness B in the next year (x varied during the course of the interview).

So the options were as follows:

Project	Age	Life expectancy	Number of people
A	20	10	10
B	10	10	X

The point X at which the subjects were indifferent between selecting projects A and B was ascertained using a slide board to visualize the person trade-off issue.

Two scenarios presented subsequently were identical to the one described above, except that the patients affected were sixty-year-olds versus twenty-year-olds and eighty-year-olds versus twenty-year-olds. Then followed a similar set of three paired comparisons involving health-improving treatments (rather than life-extending interventions). The patients in each comparison were described as "partly bedridden and in slight pain." Respondents were told that, with treatment, the patients in both age groups would live in normal health for ten years.

Results are given in Tables 9 and 10. For both life-extending and health-improving treatments, subjects gave higher preference to projects directed at younger patients. For example, extending the lives of four twenty-year-olds was considered equivalent to extending the lives of ten sixty-year-olds by the same amount (Table 9, penultimate line). The preference for the young is more pronounced the greater the disparity in the two age groups.

Table 9. *Life-extending interventions (for other people)*

Age of recipient		Equivalent numbers of people helped			
Group A	*Group B*	*A*		*B (median)*	*IQR (B)*
20-yr.-old	10-yr.-old	10	=	9.5	9.0–10.0
60-yr.-old	20-yr.-old	10	=	4.0	2.0–5.5
80-yr.-old	20-yr.-old	10	=	1.0	0.02–2.4

Table 10. *Health-improving interventions (for other people)*

Age of recipient		Equivalent numbers of people helped			
Group A	Group B	A		B (median)	IQR (B)
20-yr.-old	10-yr.-old	10	=	9.0	4.5–9.5
60-yr.-old	20-yr.-old	10	=	4.0	1.0–6.0
80-yr.-old	20-yr.-old	10	=	1.0	0.02–2.5

This study lends support to the strength with which the QALY approach favors programs for the young over programs for the elderly. However, it should be kept in mind that it was a small study, conducted in one particular country, and using a valuation technique, namely the person trade-off, which like all other valuation techniques could have biases (Nord 1995). The results were in conflict with the results from a preceding survey in which a large majority of respondents had rejected the idea of giving priority to the young over the elderly when asked about this at an ordinal level (Nord and Richardson et al. 1995). Similarly, Johannesson and Johansson (1996) acknowledge that their findings of public preferences in Sweden for giving priority to the young over the elderly were in conflict with guidelines suggested earlier by a broad government commission. Moreover, as noted above, the ordinal evidence in general varies across countries. Overall, it seems difficult to claim that the strength with which the QALY model assigns more value to helping the young than the elderly is consistent with societal preferences. The model may be correct in this respect, but it could also be wrong. At present we just don't know.

4.14 THE IMPORTANCE OF COST/THE NUMBER OF PEOPLE HELPED

In the QALY approach, the societal value of a health-care program is proportional to the number of people who get to enjoy a given health improvement. If the goal is to maximize societal value, this is the same as saying that patients should receive a priority rating that is inversely proportional to their treatment cost. For example, if patients of type A are twice as costly to treat as patients of type B, then, in order to maximize societal value, the health care system should choose As rather than Bs if, and only if, the outcome in each A is considered more than twice as valuable as the outcome in each B. Correspondingly, among patients in whom outcomes are equally valuable, the less expensive to treat should have priority.

Less emphasis is often placed on costs in the health sector than economists would deem appropriate. The story of the Oregon experiment is interesting in this respect. It was a concern for the costs of Medicaid that led to the initial attempt to draw up a priority list based on the ranking of condition-treatment pairs according to their cost per QALY. When the first list elicited highly critical public reactions, it was concluded that too much emphasis had been placed on costs (Hadorn 1991). This inference was questioned by other writers, as the counterintuitive results could be linked to flaws in the benefit measure being used (Eddy 1991; Nord 1993c). Nevertheless, the Health Services Commission in Oregon published a revised list of priorities a year later, based on a different ranking procedure in which costs played only a minor role.

Hadorn defended disregarding costs when determining priorities among health services by citing the "Rule of Rescue," a principle initially formulated by Jonsen (1986). According to Hadorn, "any plan to distribute health care services must take human nature into account if the plan is to be acceptable to society. In this regard there is a fact about the human psyche that will inevitably trump the utilitarian rationality that is implicit in cost-effectiveness analysis: people cannot stand idly by when an identified person's life is visibly threatened if rescue measures are available." According to Jonsen, "even the most evangelical utilitarian would find it difficult to expunge the rule of rescue from the psychological dynamics of technology assessors" (p. 174). Hadorn adds that "although the Rule of Rescue clearly is most compelling in the context of life saving interventions, it is also a factor whenever an identified patient is in need of treatment (e.g. for a fractured arm)."

In the following we shall look more closely at the results from a two-stage study in which a cross-section of Australians were questioned about the importance of costs in prioritizing in health-care services. I present the details of this study to enable readers to judge its validity and fully appreciate the firmness with which ordinary people reject the idea that the societal value of a health-care program is proportional to the number of people treated.

The first stage of the study was part of a general postal survey about prioritizing in health care in a sample of 2,000 people across Australia (Nord and Richardson et al. 1995). There were 551 usable responses, of which 440 were from the city of Melbourne. One of the questions in the survey presented the following options:

1. Among patients who are equally ill, those who can be helped at low cost should have priority over those who can be helped at high cost, because this will allow more people to be helped when money is limited.
2. It is unfair to discriminate against those who happen to have a high-cost illness. Priority should therefore not depend on the cost of treatment (except in cases were costs are extremely high).

The subjects were asked to indicate the view that came closest to their own. In the preface to the question, subjects were asked to assume that the patients were the same except for the difference in cost. Consequently, the first option would be selected if cost-effectiveness was the sole criterion. Eighty-one percent chose the second option, rejecting cost as an important criterion for assigning priority. Of these, 82 percent made the choice with only slight or no difficulty.

Prima facie, these results represent a decisive rejection of the assumption in the QALY procedure that societal value is proportional to the number of people treated. However, it was hypothesized that the results might have been influenced by the questionnaire design, by framing effects, and/or by the respondents' inadequate appreciation of the implications of their choices. Respondents might have disregarded the instructions and assumed that high-cost treatments produced greater benefits.

To test these hypotheses, a stage 2 of the study was conducted: A subsample of 119 of the subjects who had participated in the postal survey were interviewed personally about their views on the role of costs in prioritizing (Nord and Richardson et al. 1995b). Forty-five of these were first presented with the same options once more. Thirty-five out of these 45 (78 percent) chose option 2 (equal priority). Thirty-eight other subjects in the subsample were presented with a modified version of the cost question, in which the preface drew greater attention to the budget limitation: "Consider a situation in which a given hospital budget is to be spent on treating different groups of patients. The groups are equally ill. But the cost of treatment varies between the groups. Which of the following comes closest to your view?"

The options then presented were the same as those presented in the postal survey (see above), except that the words "should have priority" in option 1 were replaced by the weaker expression "should have some priority." It was hypothesized that, in the modified version, option 1 would be a more obvious choice. The result was that 30 percent chose to favor the low cost patients, as compared with 22 percent in the original version. The difference is not statistically significant. A clear majority of 70 percent still preferred the equal priority option.

Those who chose the equal priority option in stage 2, either in the simple retest or with the modified question (62 subjects), were challenged further about their position: "It seems inescapable that if money is limited, then it would be possible to help more people if some priority were given to those who are inexpensive to treat. Still you chose the second view. Can you explain a little further how you think about this?"

In their answers, the respondents emphasized that people cannot be blamed for contracting high-cost illnesses, that severity of illness should count rather than cost, and that people are equally entitled to treatment irrespective of cost.

The respondents were then asked: "So this is your view even if fewer people would be treated and your own chances of benefiting would be smaller?"

Nobody changed his/her mind, and several explicitly accepted the consequences in terms of a reduced chance for themselves to benefit personally.

All 119 subjects in stage 2 were then presented with a numerical example that made it clearer how different rules for prioritizing between low-cost and high-cost patients would affect the numbers of patients treated as well as the chances of any one individual receiving treatment if he or she should fall ill. Subjects were told that the treatments were equally effective and then asked which prioritizing rule they preferred in light of these explicit implications, after having been presented with brief arguments in favor of each rule. Frame 2 shows the first part of this exercise, where the choice was between Rule A, where resources are allocated to the less expensive patients, and Rule B, where spending is determined on a first-come, first serve basis.

The interview results are summarized in Table 11 under the heading Frame 2. Rule B (first-come, first-serve) was preferred to rule A (spend all money on low-cost patients) by 82 (69 percent) of the 119 interviewees.

Frame 2. Choosing between rules for allocating resources between high-cost and low-cost patients

E1. Imagine two illnesses, X and Y. People get them through no fault of their own. The illnesses are equally serious and leave the patients in a state of severe disability if untreated. They both occur in about a hundred people per year in your country. You yourself are equally likely to get either of them.

Basic care is offered to everybody who gets either of the illnesses. Beyond this basic care are treatments available for both illnesses that are equally effective and will improve the patients' functioning considerably. The treatment costs, however, depend on the illness:

Illness X: $20,000 per patient
Illness Y: $100,000 per patient

Imagine that society decides to allocate one million dollars per year to these treatments. This is not enough to treat all patients, so a rule must be established as to who should have priority. Two different rules are suggested. Rule A would be to spend all the money on people with illness X. This would lead to the following numbers of people being treated per year.

X: 50
Y: 0
Sum: 50

Rule B would be "first come, first serve." On average, this would lead to the following number of people being treated per year.

X: 10
Y: 8
Sum: 18

Advocates of rule A argue that it would allow more people to be treated and thus, all in all, lead to less disability and suffering in the population. It would also give each of us a better chance of actually benefiting one day, since more people would be treated and the illnesses are equally common.

(Frame continues on next page.)

(Frame 2 continued)

Advocates of rule B argue that it is unfair to discriminate against those who happen to get a high-cost illness through no fault of their own. They argue that this concern for fairness should override the concern for treating as many as possible. The two groups should therefore be treated on a first come, first serve basis, even though fewer people would then be treated.

You yourself are a member of the society in which one of these rules would apply. Which of them would you vote for? Take a look at this summary and think carefully before you answer (rules and consequences were shown).

Table 11. *Choices between three allocation rules*

Frame 2			Frame 3					
A vs. B	*Number*	*%*	*A vs. C*	*Number*	*%*	*B vs. C*	*Number*	*%*
A	37	(31)	A	17	(46)	B	39	(48)
B	82	(69)	C	20	(54)	C	43	(52)
Total	119	(100)		37	(100)		82	(100)

A third compromise, Rule C, was then presented to the same subjects, suggesting that priority should be given to low-cost patients, but that some capacity should be allowed for the treatment of high-cost patients (see Frame 3).

As may be seen in Table 11, of the 37 interviewees who originally chose Rule A, 54 percent opted for Rule C (some priority to low-cost patients) when this was offered in Frame 3. Similarly, 52 percent of those who initially chose Rule B over Rule A later selected Rule C when it was presented. Overall, Rule C was the preferred choice, being selected by 63 (53 percent) of the 119 subjects; 39 subjects (33 percent) preferred Rule B even to Rule C, that is, they rejected giving priority on the bases of cost. Only 17 subjects (14 percent) preferred rule A to both B and C. In other words, only a small minority would maximize the health benefits by spending all the money on the low-cost patients.

Frame 3. A possible compromise allocation rule

E2. A third rule, C, is suggested. The advocates of this rule argue that it would be unfair to exclude any patient group completely from the possiblity of receiving treatment. They also argue that by assuring everybody some chance of treatment there would always be hope whatever illness one contracted, and this would be valuable in itself. They therefore suggest that priority should be given to patients with illness X but that some capacity should be allowed for the treatment of patients with illness Y.

Again, as a member of the society in which one of these rules would apply, of rules C and A or B which would you vote for?

Finally, those who preferred Rule C were shown five possible ways of dividing the budget between the high-cost and the low-cost groups (the "production frontier") and asked which of these outcomes they would select (see Frame 4).

Results are given in Table 12. Of the 63 subjects who selected Rule C, 30 (48 percent) chose option III for dividing a given budget between two illnesses, as specified in Frame 4. This option entails that of the 50 patients whom it would be possible to treat, 34 are actually treated. Seventeen subjects (27 percent) chose option II, in which a total of 26 patients receive treatment.

The bottom line is that *94 percent of the 119 subjects in this study preferred to allocate the budget in a way that did not maximize the number of patients who would be treated.* The reliability and validity of this result have been discussed elsewhere (Nord and Richardson et al. 1995b). It is hard to imagine that the implications of different choices could be made more clearly than in the numerical examples used in this study. In sum, there seems little reason to doubt that the preferences observed in the study for equity between high-cost and low-cost patients were firmly held by well-informed subjects. There was also little variation in the pattern of response by age, socioeconomic status, or previous health history, suggesting that using a different group of respondents would not have altered the main conclusions.

Frame 4. Possible combinations of patients treated

The table below shows some possible combinations of numbers of people treated if total expenditure were limited to one million dollars per year.

Again, as a member of the society in which rule C would apply, which of these combinations would you vote for? Please consider both the argument that one should treat as many as possible and, on the other hand, the argument that both groups should have some chance of being treated.

Illness	Numbers treated per year					Number of cases per year
	I	II	III	IV	V	
X	10	20	30	40	50	100
Y	8	6	4	2	0	100
Totals	18	26	34	42	50	

Table 12. *Preferences for the distribution of resources across high-cost and low-cost patients*

	Allocation of US $1 million to two illnesses				
	Frame 4 Numbers treated under each option				
Illness	I	II	III	IV	V
X	10	20	30	40	50
Y	8	6	4	2	0
Total	18	26	34	42	50
	Number (%) of subjects selecting each option				
	3 (5)	17 (27)	30 (48)	9 (14)	4 (6)

Economists will tend to regard these observed preferences as irrational, on the ground that it cannot be in anybody's interest to vote for prioritization rules that would reduce everybody's chances of receiving treatment in case of illness. However, it is possible to envisage a rational basis for these preferences as the result of three possible sources of indirect utility, that is, utility that arises from the process by which health care is delivered as distinct from the health-related outcome.

First, despite the objective fact that more people may be treated and more health be obtained by cost-based discrimination, repondents might consider the existence of a *chance* of treatment in serious states of illness to be of importance, even if the chance is small. This is consistent with the preference by many respondents for Rule C, which explicitly included this argument (see Frame 3). In effect, a limited number of treatments offered to patients in a given state of illness creates a rational basis for hope: no matter what health-related event occurs, respondents know there is a chance of treatment, and hope is a rational basis for utility.

A second source of (dis)utility may arise if respondents anticipate their own emotional response if they were to be seriously ill and were refused treatment despite resources being available, albeit at a high cost. While some patients might be phlegmatic and say to themselves: "Fair enough, I accept that I am the unlucky one who does not qualify for treatment because I happen to be costly to treat," many might not react in such a self-disciplined manner. Analogously, some people might accept an explicit explanation from their family doctor that he or she would not be offered treatment because the societal cost of the treatment was too great. However, we would expect that most people would feel frustrated and resentful in such a situation. The data may indicate that most people have a similar feeling in a less personal decision-making context, namely, that of deciding admission policies across diagnostic groups. The anticipation of such feelings might lead respondents rationally to precommit the system to the treatment of cases where nontreatment might lead to feelings of resentment and anger.

A third and closely related source of utility is the Rule of Rescue. This is the sense of immediate duty that people feel toward those who present themselves to a health service with a serious condition. This sense of duty may lead people to feel that a society is callous or uncaring if it withholds expensive treatments when resources are available at the moment of demand. To follow this sense of duty may lead to waiting in line and fewer people being treated, but these consequences may not be considered as undesirable as withholding possible treatment from those in great need. Such subjective feelings are a legitimate basis for utility.

I conclude that although the assumption in the QALY approach that societal value is proportional to the number of people treated has an undeniable intuitive appeal it has no empirical basis. The evidence that exists, in countries as far apart as Norway and Australia, suggests that most people are prepared to make quite significant sacrifices in terms of the total number of people treated by the health-care system in order to allow the system to treat fairly those who happen to have a high-cost illness. This has potentially far reaching implications for the relevance of cost-effectiveness analysis in resource allocation decisions. I shall return to this in the final chapter.

4.15 THE IMPORTANCE OF THE CHANCE OF SUCCESSFUL TREATMENT

Medical outcomes are surrounded by uncertainty. Health gains of interventions in terms of QALYs are therefore calculated in terms of *statistically expected gains*. In the simplest case, where the intervention is either a 100 percent success or a 100 percent failure, the expected gain is the product of the QALYs gained if the intervention is successful and the probability of success. For instance, if a successful intervention provides twenty QALYs, and seven out of ten interventions of this kind are successful, then the statistically expected benefit of the intervention is $20 \times 0.7 = 14$ QALYs. In the QALY approach, the societal value of an intervention is thus proportional to the probability of success.

Although there is a long tradition of physicians' emphasizing the probability of success in medical decision making at the admission and bedside levels, there have been few studies of societal attitudes regarding the role that this factor should play in resource allocation decisions. A notable exception is a study by Ubel and Loewenstein (1995). They asked 138 subjects to (hypothetically) distribute scarce livers among transplant candidates with either a 70 percent chance or a 30 percent chance of surviving. They found that while the subjects were clearly inclined to give a higher percentage of the organs to the group with the better prognosis, they were equally clearly unwilling to give all the available organs to this group. The authors concluded that "most people were not solely interested in the aggregate benefit brought by different allocation systems, but were also interested in the amount of benefit brought to the worst off."

Two kinds of arguments and data presented in previous sections of this book suggest that the assumption in the QALY approach of proportionality between probability of success and societal value may be incorrect. One is the realization-of-potential concern, reflected in a reluctance to discriminate among patients that are equally ill and amenable to treatment even if they differ with respect to how much better they can become. If people value interventions for patients with different potentials more or less equally (as long as the treatment effect is substantial), then it would not be surprising if they also equally valued interventions that differed somewhat in probability of success, as long as the probability is above some critical level.

The other observation that gives reason to question the probability of success assumption in the QALY approach is the finding that people do not seem to assign value to programs in a way that is proportional to the number of people treated. To see the connection, imagine a health service that is considering how to distribute a million dollars to three patient categories A, B, and C, as in the table below. Successful treatment provides ten QALYs per patient in each category. The probability of success is 1.0 in A and B, but only 0.3 in C. The costs per patient are US$50,000 in A and C, US$100,000 in B.

Patient category	QALY gain per patient if successful	Probability of success	Cost per treatment (US$)
A	10	1.0	50,000
B	10	1.0	100,000
C	10	0.3	50,000

Let us first consider a choice between spending the budget only on A and/or B. If the cost factor is fully emphasized, as the QALY approach suggests, then interventions in A will be preferable to interventions in B. Spending the whole budget on A will yield 200 QALYs (20 people, 10 QALYs each). By contrast, if the cost differential between A and B is disregarded, and A and B hence are given equal priority, the budget will allow the treatment of roughly 6 people in A and 7 people in B ($6 \times 50,000 + 7 \times 100,000 = 1,000,000$), resulting in 130 QALYs gained (13 people, 10 QALYs each). So if society rejects the cost factor, it will in this case be accepting a loss of 70 QALYs

(200–130) in order to treat fairly those who happen to have a high-cost illness.

Now let us compare this with a choice between spending the budget only on A and/or C. If the probability-of-success factor is fully emphasized, as the QALY approach suggests, then interventions in A will be preferable to interventions in C. Spending the whole budget on A will again yield 200 QALYs (20 people, 10 QALYs each). By contrast, if the probability differential between A and C is disregarded, and A and C hence are given equal priority, the budget will allow the treatment of 10 people in A and 10 people in C (10 × 50,000 + 10 × 50,000 = 1,000,000), resulting in 130 QALYs gained (10 × 10 + 10 × 10 × 0.3). So if society rejected the probability factor, it would be accepting a loss of 70 QALYs (200 − 130) in order to treat fairly those who happen to have a low probability of success. This means that the consequences – in terms of lost QALYs – of disregarding the probability factor and the cost factor are the same in this example. The question is then: Is there any reason why society should be more prepared to discriminate against those who happen to be *cost-ineffective* to treat when the reason for the cost-ineffectiveness is low probability of success rather than high cost?

One reason could be that probability of success is a medical aspect of the decision problem and is therefore intuitively perceived by the public as an inherently germane, legitimate aspect. Cost, on the other hand, is a nonmedical aspect that many may find more difficult to accept as legitimate, even if its importance for the actual production of health within a given budget is no less than the importance of the probability-of-success factor.

But it could also be that the emphasis being placed on the probability-of-success factor in medical decision making derives, not from societal preferences in general, but rather from physicians' personal preferences in their daily work. Clearly, working with patients in whom significant health improvements are achieved is psychologically more rewarding than working with those in whom interventions fail to have beneficial effects. This is a perfectly understandable preference on the part of physicians. But it can hardly carry much weight in guiding resource allocation decisions, as the aim of health insurance schemes (public or private) is not to maximize value for their employees, but rather for their members (be they patients or the public at large).

In conclusion, it is not clear that the assumption in the QALY approach of proportionality between the probability of success of an intervention, on the one hand, and its societal value, on the other, is valid. Further empirical research is needed to clarify this issue.

4.16 SUMMARY

This chapter has addressed the assumption of distributive neutrality in the QALY approach. I have argued that this assumption violates a number of societal concerns for fairness in the allocation of health-care resources. First, it overlooks the high degree to which people wish to give priority to the severely ill over the less severely ill at the expense of the total amount of health produced. Here the empirical evidence is substantial, suggesting a dramatic degree of error in existing instruments for evaluating health states for resource allocation purposes. Second, the QALY approach overlooks a societal concern for allowing people to realize their potential for health, whether this is big or small. This implies less discrimination than is suggested by the QALY approach between groups of patients with different capacities to benefit from a given treatment. The concern for the realization of potentials for health is best documented with respect to improvements in functioning and quality of life. But data also suggest that the QALY assumption of proportionality or close-to-proportionality between duration of benefits and societal value is exaggerated. Third, it is unclear whether the strength with which the QALY model assigns more value to treating the young than the elderly is consistent with societal preferences when both concerns for duration and age per se are taken into account. Fourth, the QALY assumption of proportionality between the number of people treated and societal value is exaggerated. Fifth, the validity of the assumption of proportionality between probability of success and societal value is unclear.

The empirical data underlying these propositions were mostly collected within a caring-for-others perspective. However, some studies adopted a self-interest perspective behind a veil of ignorance. Overall, data collected in these two different perspectives tend to support each other.

It is on the basis of these observations that I contend that to rank projects in terms of costs-per-QALY as often as not may tend to distort resource allocation decisions rather than to inform and aid them.

4.17 ARE BETTER WEIGHTS OR ADDITIONAL EQUITY WEIGHTS A SOLUTION?

What the above criticisms basically mean is that the weights used in QALY calculations do not capture societal values correctly. Could, then, the QALY approach be made more valid simply by using more appropriate weights?

Two possibilities are worth mentioning here. One, noted briefly earlier, is to replace utilities based on healthy people's hypothetical valuations of health states with utilities elicited directly from patients (Emmett Keeler, personal communication). As will be shown in Chapter 5, the latter tend to have much stronger upper-end compression than the former, and this would fit better with the upper-end compression of health-state scores that is required to model societal concerns for severity and realization of potentials for health in resource allocation decisions.

Another possibility, suggested by Culyer (1989) and Williams (1988b; 1994; 1997), is to add "equity weights" to the QALY model. If society values utility gains differently depending on who gets them, then this may be incorporated in the QALY approach by assigning weights to utility gains that reflect relevant characteristics of the recipients of the gains.

In his own work, Williams (1997) has primarily focused on characteristics like age, sex, and socioeconomic status. As noted in section 4.2, he argues that the *fair innings argument* – that is, the general sentiment that everyone is entitled to a "normal" lifetime of around 70–75 years – is a salient ethical basis for the introduction of equity weights. He goes on to present a hypothetical table of equity weights for QALYs that could be used in comparisons of programs for socioeconomic groups that differ with respect to quality-adjusted life expectancy at birth.

Although Williams's approach is interesting, it aims only at incorporating the fair-innings argument into economic evaluation. It does not resolve the problems with societal concerns for giving priority on the basis of severity of condition and for not discriminating very strongly among patients with different potentials for health improvements. However, it certainly is possible to introduce equity weights to encapsulate these concerns as well. To see this, let us go back to the rules of thumb that apply for scoring health states if QALY calculations are to capture societal preferences for resource allocation across patient groups with different degrees of severity of their condition:

Degree of severity	Suggested value
Moderate problem	0.99
Considerable problem	0.92
Severe problem	0.75
Life-threatening condition	0.00

Let us assume that an analyst uses the York EuroQol TTO tariff to assign utilities to these states. The result is as follows:

Degree of severity	Suggested value
Moderate problem	0.80
Considerable problem	0.45
Severe problem	0.20
Life-threatening condition	0.00

The QALY gain per year obtained by curing a person in these different conditions would be:

Degree of severity	According to rules of thumb	According to utilities
Moderate problem	0.01	0.20
Considerable problem	0.08	0.55
Severe problem	0.25	0.80
Life-threatening condition	1.00	1.00

The QALY gains calculated on the basis of individual utilities (second column) would, in other words, be highly incorrect if the purpose is to express societal values (first column). However, QALY calculations using individual utilities would become roughly right if the gains in terms of utility were multiplied by fractions reflecting the degree of severity at the outset:

Degree of severity	Utility gains	$\times$	Severity	$= QALY$
Moderate problem	0.20	$\times$	$1/20$	$= 0.01$
Considerable problem	0.55	$\times$	$1/7$	$= 0.08$
Severe problem	0.80	$\times$	$1/3$	$= 0.27$
Life-threatening condition	1.00	$\times$	1	$= 1.00$

So, technically, it is feasible to supplement the present utility-oriented QALY model with an additional weight for the severity of the initial condition, so that the outcome of a QALY calculation fits with societal preferences for resource allocation as summarized in the Rules of Thumb. Two different ways of doing this have been published elsewhere. Dolan (1998), building on Wagstaff (1991), asked subjects to judge directly the trade-off between the severity of the initial condition and the size of the health gain (see details in section 4.5). Nord et al. (1999) suggest that severity weights may be estimated by asking people to make person trade-offs between movements that are equal in terms of utility gains. Similarly, they suggest that potential weights may be estimated by asking people to make person trade-offs between movements that are equal in terms of severity (start point), but different in terms of utility gains. Details of these procedures are given in the appendix to this chapter.

It should be noted that the approach advocated by Wagstaff, Williams, and Dolan is not applicable to establishing potential weights (see appendix).

Nord et al. (1999) note that, even if concerns for fairness in theory may be taken into account by means of severity weights and potential weights, there is a danger that the introduction of such weights will make economic valuation models look extremely complicated, academic, and farfetched to practically oriented decision makers. Empirical research among potential users is needed to establish the degree to which this may be true. Irrespective of this psychological problem, there remains a more fundamental difficulty with equity-weighted QALYs. It has to do with the concept of utility itself and with difficulties in measuring utility at a cardinal level. In the next chapter I address this issue.

APPENDIX. SEVERITY WEIGHTS AND POTENTIAL WEIGHTS DERIVED BY MEANS OF THE PERSON TRADE-OFF

For severity weights, consider, for instance, the following three movements on the utility scale:

Movement	Utility
X	$0.0 \rightarrow 0.3$
Y	$0.3 \rightarrow 0.6$
Z	$0.6 \rightarrow 0.9$

Subjects would be asked questions of the following kind: In judging different areas in which to increase treatment capacity, how many Ys would be equivalent to 10 Xs? How many Zs would be equivalent to 10 Xs? Assume that the median answers to these questions were: 10X = 20Y; 10 = 50Z. If the severity weight for X (life saving) was set at 1, the severity weight for movement Y would be $1 \times (10{:}20) = 0.5$. The severity weight for movement Z would be $1 \times (10{:}50) = 0.2$.

A potential weight (PW) may be operationalized in various ways. Nord et al. (1999) focus on the ratio

$$(U_2 - U_1) / (1 - U_1)$$

which expresses the ratio between actual potential for a given patient group with utility levels U_1 and U_2, respectively, before and after treatment, and the greatest possible potential for health in patients with initial utility level U_1. This is called the *relative potential ratio (RPR)*. PW would be set at 1 for $U_2 = 1$ (largest possible potential) to ensure that the societal value scale would have unity as its maximum value, just like the conventional individual utility scale. PW would *increase* with falling values of the relative potential ratio, so that small utility gains would be assigned added importance relative to bigger utility gains in the estimate of societal value.

To see the mathematics of potential weights, consider, for instance, the following three movements on the utility scale:

Movement	Utility	Relative Potential Ratio
X	$0.4 \rightarrow 0.6$	1/3
Y	$0.4 \rightarrow 0.8$	2/3
Z	$0.4 \rightarrow 1.0$	1/1

Subjects would be asked person trade-off questions of the following kind: In judging different areas in which to increase treatment capacity, how many Ys would be equivalent to 10 Zs? How many Xs would be equivalent to 10 Zs? Assume that the median answers to these questions were: 10Z = 13Y; 10Z = 20X. As noted above, the potential weight for Z would be set at 1. The potential weight (PW) for movement Y – for which RPR equals 2/3 – would then be given by

$$13 * (0.8 - 0.4) * PW_Y = 10 * (1.0 - 0.4) * PW_Z$$

where $PW_Z = 1$, such that

$$PW_Y = 1.15$$

This could then be used as a potential weight for movements for which RPR equals 2/3. Similarly, the potential weight for movement X – for which RPR equals 1/3 – would be given by:

$$20 * (0.6 - 0.4) * PW_x = 10 * (1.0 - 0.4) * PW_z$$
$$PW_x = 1.5$$

This could then be used as a potential weight for movements for which RPR equals 1/3.

It should be noted that the approach advocated by Wagstaff, Williams, and Dolan is not applicable to establishing potential weights. (The following clearly does *not* do the trick: "Assume that A and B are both at utility level 0.4. A can be taken to 0.8, while B can be taken to 0.6. To what utility level must it be possible to take B for you to give the two patients equal priority?")

Chapter 5

The Limitations of Utility Measurement

There are a highly worrisome subjectivity and diversity in the ways in which the QALY gains of different interventions are calculated in applied health economics. For instance, in a review of fifteen published studies, I found that twenty-four out of thirty-six valuations of health states were based simply on the various authors' own rough judgments of what seemed to be "reasonable" or "plausible" values. Seven were taken from previous publications. In one of these seven cases, no reference was given. In another, the valuation could not be found in the reference that was given. In two cases, the value in the previous publications was based on its author's own judgment. In the remaining three cases, the values turned out to be based on a scale that does not purport to be a utility scale (Nord 1993e). Gerard (1992) and Salkeld et al. (1995) report similar findings.

A reason for this unsatisfactory situation seems to be a considerable lack of consensus in the scientific community as to what exactly QALYs are supposed to count (Richardson 1994). There is of course an agreement in general terms, as reflected in the elementary explanation given in Chapter 3. But a genuinely curious person who wonders exactly what utility numbers and QALYs correspond to in the real world is likely to get many different answers.

In the following I shall discuss the meaning and the measurement of utilities in considerable detail. There are many thorny issues here. I concentrate on the following:

1. Are utilities meant to be ex ante or ex post?
2. Whom should one ask about the utility of health states?
3. How should one ask?

4. Difficulties in capturing the utility of minor and moderate improvements in health.
5. Is the utility of a life-saving intervention a finite number?

I stress that any calculation of gains in utility presupposes that one knows the actual medical effects of the service in question in terms of gained functioning, quality of life, and duration of benefit. This is often *not* the case. On the contrary, there is increasing recognition that a large part of modern medical practice is based on physicians' traditions and beliefs rather than on scientific evidence of procedures' beneficial effects (Sackett et al. 1997). This measurement problem on the medical side often makes economic evaluation in terms of QALYs futile. However, here I leave this problem aside and concentrate on problems with measuring the utility of given medical outcomes.

5.1 EX ANTE OR EX POST UTILITIES?

As noted in Chapter 3, the utility of a health state is the same as the goodness of it to the individuals who are in it. The utility gain that follows from a medical treatment is then the difference between the goodness of the pre-treatment and the post-treatment state. This goodness may be judged ex ante, that is before the treatment, or ex post, that is after the treatment. While these judgments may coincide (Llewellyn-Thomas et al. 1993), one cannot assume that they always will. Clearly, individuals may come to perceive states of illness in ways that differ from what they thought the states would be like before they had any personal experience with them.

In the QALY literature, it is not always clear which of these judgments utilities are supposed to reflect, as the terms "ex ante utility" and "ex post utility" are rarely used. However, Weinstein and Stason (1977) describe a way of measuring utility as follows: "Taking into account your age, pain and suffering, immobility, and lost earnings, what fraction, P, of a year of life would you be willing to give up to be completely healthy for the remaining fraction of a year instead of your present level of health status for the full year?" (p. 719). Here the authors clearly have ex post utility in mind. Other writers stress that utilities for health states should be elicited from *informed* representative population samples (Torrance 1986; Gold et al. 1996). Being "informed" then means knowing how conditions of illness are felt by those who are in them, in other words, knowing the ex post utilities.

In the following I shall judge procedures for eliciting utilities on the assumption that utilities used in QALY calculations need to be elicited ex post. The rationale for this is as follows. The QALY approach is basically an attempt to evaluate the outcomes of health services. As such it is an empirical discipline. It tries to capture what actually happens in different areas of health care and to feed this information back to decision makers in order to aid future decisions about resource allocation. In doing this, the QALY approach shares the basic idea of evidence based medicine (see, e.g., Sackett et al. 1997): that medical practice should be based on documented effects rather than on traditions and assumptions.

This has two implications. On the one hand, QALY calculations should be based on the examination of data from interventions that have actually taken place. This includes data on the goodness of the end states as these were experienced by the individuals involved – in other words, ex post utilities. On the other hand, QALY calculations are meant to serve as aids in ex ante judgments of health-care programs. These ex ante judgments may include concerns for other factors than health benefits observed ex post. Two such factors are particularly worth mentioning. One is the uncertainty of outcomes for patients undergoing a procedure. Patients tend to dislike uncertainty, and particularly to be aversive to risk (Kahneman and Tversky 1983). Uncertainty is a normal aspect of medical practice but of course, mainly an ex ante aspect; ex post, patients generally know how things went. The other factor is distance in time until the outcome occurs. Say, for instance, that an intervention is expected to increase an individual's life expectancy from ten to twelve years. Because of the distance in time, the added two years may, ex ante, be judged less valuable to the individual than what is suggested by the ex post utilities of these years, that is, the utility associated with them when they actually occur.

To see, then, the different elements of a QALY calculation that purports to capture the societal value of proposed programs, consider an intervention that increases individuals' life expectancy from ten to twelve years, where the two added years are either in state A or state B, with probabilities p and $(1-p)$ and ex post utilities U(A) and U(B), respectively. The expected value of the ex post utility (E) of each of the years added by the intervention is then

$$E = p \times U(A) + (1-p) \times U(B) \qquad (1)$$

This expected value corresponds to the average ex post utility in a large number of individuals receiving the intervention in question. It may be estimated on the basis of historical data.

The *ex ante societal value* of the intervention, measured in QALYs gained, is:

$$QALY = E \times 2 \times R \times T \qquad (2)$$

where the number 2 stands for 2 added years, R is a discount factor encapsulating that the outcome of the intervention is uncertain, and T is a discount factor encapsulating that the utility gain is ten years in the future.

The distinction I make here between utility measurement and QALY measurement is essential. QALYs are supposed to aid ex ante judgments of health-care programs. However, they are most helpful if they are based on data from real experiences with illness, namely, utilities measured ex post. The QALY estimate of an outcome may then be interpreted as the value that people with true insight ("informed subjects," in the terminology of Gold et al. 1996) ex ante place on that outcome when they think about it as something they themselves are to experience. The inclusion of aversion to risk and discounting for distance in time in ex ante judgments of health interventions does not eliminate the need to measure ex post utilities as a step to estimating actual health benefits of medical activities.

When I use the term "utility" in the following, it will be in the ex post sense. I shall at a later point return to the issue of assessing health interventions ex ante given the fact that people have aversion to risk and preference for present over future events.

5.2 WHOM TO ASK

5.2.1 *The Prima Facie Case for Asking Patients*

As noted earlier, the utility of a health state is, broadly speaking, the health-related quality of life that people in that state personally experience. This is the same as ex post utility. One would think that the best source of information about this personal experience must be those people themselves. In other words, if you want to know the utility (or disutility, rather) of severe asthma, ask people with severe asthma (or who have had severe asthma).

This is not the approach normally adopted in utility assessment today. Most utilities are elicited from subjects who are asked to imagine themselves in various states of illness and to indicate the degree of disutility they think they would experience in each of these states (for a review, see Nord 1992a).

There are good reasons for this practice in terms of convenience. First, it allows researchers to use subjects in their immediate surroundings, such as colleagues and students. These are not only easier to access than patients but often also easier to induce into participating in a study. Second, a person can imagine himself or herself in a number of different states but actually be in only one of them at a given point in time. To cover the same number of health states a researcher using patients' self-reports would therefore have to elicit valuations from many more subjects than a researcher satisfying himself or herself with a group of people's multiple hypothetical valuations.

Nonetheless, a serious concern arising from current practice is whether people can be expected to know what it is like to be in health states that they have never experienced.

Defenders of hypothetical valuations may argue that, in hypothetical valuation exercises, health states are described not in terms of diagnoses but rather in terms of concrete symptoms and functional impairments. The subjects need therefore not be familiar with specific illnesses. They only need to know the disutility of such health problems as not being able to walk, work, or dress, and so on, or of having pain, nausea, sleeplessness, and so on. Arguably, these are dysfunctions which most people are able to judge on the basis of personal experience at sometime in their lives. There is empirical support of this assumption with respect to short-term health states (Llewellyn-Thomas et al. 1993).

The problem, however, is the time factor. Clinical decision-making and resource allocation decisions are often about helping patients with chronic or potentially chronic conditions. The impact on quality of life of long-lasting but stable dysfunctions may be quite different from the effects of temporary disruptive illness episodes experienced by otherwise healthy people. The difference may cut both ways. On the one hand, patients may become mentally worn out and increasingly frustrated by long-lasting illness (Sutherland et al. 1982). On the other hand, chronically ill people may, over time, learn to adjust their expectations and to cope with situations that at first seemed difficult or hopeless (Calman 1984; Knussen and Cunningham 1988).

What, then, do the data tell us about patients' experiences with different states of illness and other people's evaluation of these states?

5.2.2 *Data on Patients' Quality of Life*

A first difficulty is variability in the way in which illness affects quality of life. The significance of this factor is indicated in a study by Spitzer et al. (1981). They used the Quality of Life Index to score: (*a*) a group of mainly healthy people who consulted general practitioners for trivial or temporary conditions; (*b*) patients with severe chronic diseases such as rheumatoid arthritis, advanced diabetes, spinal injury, or chronic obstructive lung disease; (*c*) patients with the most common kinds of cancer; and (*d*) critically or terminally ill patients. The instrument includes the following dimensions: activity (employment, studying, housework), everyday life (moving about and self-care), health (self-assessed feeling of being healthy), support (support from and contact with family and friends), and outlook (anxiety/depression). Each dimension has three steps ($0/1/2$), so that the maximum total score is 10. The healthy had a mean score of 9.0, versus 7.3 in the chronically ill, 7.1 in the cancer patients, and 3.3 in the critically ill. Interestingly, however, 18 percent of the chronically ill obtained the maximum score (10) in spite of the severity of their condition. More than half of them scored 8 or higher, while 25 percent scored 5 or lower. Similar figures were found for the cancer patients. By contrast, in the critically or terminally ill, 80 percent of the patients scored 4 or less.

Cassileth et al. (1984) examined 758 patients with arthritis, depression, diabetes, cancer, terminal renal failure, and skin disease by means of the Mental Health Index. The index has 43 items, and the patients are scored on a scale from zero to one hundred with respect to anxiety, depression, positive affect, emotional ties, loss of control, and global mental health. On all these dimensions, mental health was found to be 10–15 percentage points higher in sixty-year-olds than in forty-year-olds in the six patient groups in question. The authors suggest that "chronic illness, ironically, offers social advantages that are less available to the healthy elderly, such as increases in activity, involvement with others, and the amount of attention and concern received. On the basis of years and experience, older people may develop more effective skills with which to manage stressful life events. Their perspective and expectations may be more commensurate with adaptation to illness than is the case for younger patients. There may be a biological, evolutionary advantage for older patients, enabling them to adapt to illnesses that are epidemiologically associated with advancing years" (p. 509).

Pearlman and Uhlmann (1988) studied 126 patients over sixty-four years old with at least one of the following chronic diseases: arthritis, ischemic heart disease, chronic lung disease, diabetes mellitus, and cancer. Patients described their global quality of life on a six-step scale ranging from "about as good as possible" to "terrible, quality of life is very poor." Differences between mean scores in the different patient groups were very small (means ranged from 2.1 to 2.4) and statistically nonsignificant, in spite of the large differences in the illnesses themselves. On average, the patients described their own health as somewhere between "good" and "fair," judged their health to be a little *better* than "average for most people of the same sex and age," and felt that their health problems affected their quality of life only a little more than "slightly."

Stewart et al. (1989) examined (*a*) 5,068 patients spread over nine chronic diseases (hypertension, diabetes, heart failure, myocardial infarction, arthritis, chronic lung disease, gastrointestinal disease, back pain, and angina); (*b*) 2,595 nonchronically ill patients; and (*c*) 2,002 people from the general population, using the Medical Outcomes Study Short-Form General Health Survey. The instrument covers physical, role and social functioning, mental health, self-assessed health, and physical pain. All variables were measured on a scale from zero to one hundred. The mental health variable includes five items concerning "general mood or affect, including depression, anxiety and positive well-being during the past month." It is thus the variable that most closely measures the psychological impact of illness. With the exception of the hypertensive, the chronically ill scored significantly poorer on all dimensions than the nonchronically ill. Interestingly, however, the differences in mean scores were much smaller on the mood dimension ("mental health") than on the other dimensions (typically 3–4 percentage points versus 10–15 percentage points).

In an explorative study, Selai and Rosser (1995) obtained quality-of-life ratings on a visual analogue scale running from zero to one hundred from twenty-three severely ill inpatients in a London hospital. The scores ranged from 30 to 100, with a mean of 64. In comparison, previous hypothetical valuations in a general population sample by means of the same visual analogue scale predict a mean score in the order of 55 (my calculation based on Williams 1995b).

In a number of studies, convenience samples of healthy people and/or patients have been asked to value health states other than their own in terms of hypothetical questions about their willingness to sacrifice life years in order to be relieved of symtoms and dysfunctions (the time trade-off technique, Torrance 1986). The following are some examples of scores that have been elicited: walking stick: 0.78; walking frame: 0.58 (Bombardier et al. 1982); moderate angina: 0.83; severe angina: 0.53 (Read et al. 1984); removed breast, unconcerned: 0.80 (Richardson et al. 1989); removed breast, occasionally concerned: 0.70 (Buxton et al. 1987); some problems with moving about: 0.85; some problems with moving about and moderate pain: 0.73 (Williams 1995b). These results may be compared with results from studies in which patients have been asked to evaluate their own health state by means of the time trade-off technique.

Churchill et al. (1984) used the technique to measure quality of life in renal patients, 42 of whom were on hemodialysis, 17 on ambulant peritoneal dialysis, and 14 who had received transplants. The variability in willingness to sacrifice longevity to become well was striking, particularly in the hemodialysis group, where there is an almost rectangular distribution ranging from 10 to 100 percent. The mean utility score in this group was 0.54.

Fryback et al. (1993) studied health-related quality of life in a random sample of 1,356 adults in a community population, using, among other instruments, a time trade-off questionnaire. Their report includes twenty-five chronic conditions that affected a sufficient number of people to allow calculations of mean TTO-scores with 95 percent confidence intervals less than 15 percentage points. The willingness to sacrifice longevity (WTSL) in order to be cured of one specific illness was not observed directly, as the TTO refers to becoming healthy and most subjects had more than one condition. However, the authors estimated that the conditions associated with the highest disutilities were insulin dependent diabetes (WTSL = 24 percent), depression (17 percent), asthma (16 percent), and chronic bronchitis (14 percent). The willingness to sacrifice was only 5–8 percent in people with arthritis, severe back pain, migraine, angina, cataracts, ulcers, colitis, and sleep disorder.

Tsevat et al. (1994) applied the time trade-off technique in 1,438 seriously ill patients with a projected overall six-month mortality rate of

50 percent. The patients had at least one of the following nine diseases: acute respiratory failure, acute exacerbation of severe chronic obstructive pulmonary disease, acute exacerbation of severe chronic congestive heart failure, chronic liver failure with cirrhosis, nontraumatic coma, colon cancer metastatic to the liver, metastatic non-small-cell carcinoma of the lung, multiorgan system failure with malignancy, and multiorgan system failure with sepsis. The subjects were asked to choose (hypothetically) between one year in the current state and a shorter time period healthy. Responses varied widely. Mean willingness to sacrifice time was 27 percent, corresponding to a utility score of 0.73. Thirty-five percent of the patients were unwilling to exchange any time in their current state for a shorter life in excellent health.

Sherbourne et al. (1997) collected time trade-off and standard gamble data from 18,000 patients visiting medical centers across the United States. On average, the patients scored themselves 75 on a rating scale from 0 ("worst possible health state") to 100 ("perfect health"). However, 70 percent of the patients, including many who were very sick, were not willing to sacrifice any life expectancy to be relieved of their condition.

In a number of studies, patients' personal judgments of their own health and quality of life have been compared directly with judgments elicited from relatives and/or health-care personnel (Nord 1992b). Some find a tendency for patients to score themselves higher than relatives and health-care personnel do (Yager and Linn 1981; Spitzer et al. 1981; Rubinstein et al. 1984; Magaziner et al. 1988; Pearlman and Uhlmann 1988; Epstein et al. 1989; Rothman et al. 1991), while others find no systematic differences (Derogatis et al. 1976; Churchill et al. 1984; McCusker and Stoddard 1984; Clipp and Elder 1987; O'Brien and Francis 1988; Slevin et al. 1988). I am not aware of studies that have reported opposite results.

While the above studies provide neither an accurate nor an exhaustive picture of quality of life in patients, some tentative conclusions may be drawn. First, the quality of life associated with a given condition varies widely. Second, chronically ill people seem to differ less from healthy people in terms of subjectively perceived well-being than one might expect by simply judging health differences. Third, the expressed disutility and the willingness to sacrifice (longevity) to be relieved of illness seems somewhat less when patients are asked to evaluate their own current health state than when healthy people are asked to evaluate different hypothetical conditions. The ability to cope and adapt to illness over time presents itself as a likely explanation of all these observations.

In sum, the above studies indicate that while it certainly is *convenient* to substitute hypothetical health-state valuations for patients' self-reported utilities, the two approaches lead to different results. Is there, in the face of the prima facie argument in favor of self-reports, any way to justify the substitution? In other words, can adherents to current practice claim that hypothetical valuations are not only more convenient but actually more on target that self-reported utilities?

I am aware of three arguments to this effect.

5.2.3 Hypothetical Valuations: Arguments and Counterarguments

One argument is that asking patients about themselves involves a risk of strategic response bias – that is, a risk that the patients, in an effort to secure more health care for themselves, will tend to exaggerate the disutility of their condition (Williams 1987a). Evidence does not suggest that this is much of a problem (Torrance 1986). Nonetheless, the hypothesis would be difficult to disregard if in fact patients' self-ratings tended to be lower than hypothetical valuations of the same states. As we have seen, it is in fact the other way around. This does not necessarily mean that strategic bias does not occur. However, since the bias calls for upward rather than downward adjustments of responses, the replacement of patients' self-ratings by hypothetical valuations can hardly be the answer.

Another argument in favor of hypothetical valuations is that policymakers may to some extent have to accommodate the beliefs of the general population – be they right or wrong – when making decisions about resource allocation. This may be true, but I don't think the argument carries very far. Not only would it be irrational for decision makers to place great emphasis on the general population's beliefs if they had reason to think that the beliefs deviated significantly from reality; we must also assume that the general population's beliefs would change if it turned out that the patients themselves felt differently and this was communicated to people in general. So, at the end of the day, I think patients' self-reports are bound to prevail (although I realize that others may think differently, see, for instance, a highly readable piece by Brock 1995). (As an aside, I would add that utilities are used not only in economic evaluation but also in monitoring health and clinical decision making. In these contexts, patients' actual perceptions of the disutility of illness must clearly be more relevant than the general population's beliefs about illness.)

A third argument against using self-reported utilities goes like this: The more people learn to cope, the less disutility they report. If societal value were proportional to the reduction in self-reported disutility, then helping people even with severe disabilities could carry little societal value, because of their ability to cope. In fact, there could be just as much value in teaching patients to cope as in reducing their symptoms and improving their functioning. This is not the kind of policy implications we want economic evaluation to have.

This argument is in a sense true. But it does not bear on the issue of utility measurement. Coping affects utility and should therefore be incorporated when utility measurement is the issue. The argument reveals a more basic problem with the QALY model. Society may very well wish to take into account *both* objective symptom relief and functional improvement *and* the increase in subjective utility (quality of life) when valuing a health service (see the list of potentially relevant factors in Chapter 1). In other words, both these factors may need to be included in the societal value function. The trouble with the QALY model is that it only includes one of them, namely subjective utility. Having made this choice, then this is also the concept the constructors of the model need to operationalize. They can, of course, try to make up for having left out something important at the conceptual level by choosing an operationalization of utility that goes beyond the underlying theoretical concept of utility. But, needless to say, that is creating a mess rather than a logical, scientific structure. The solution to the problem posed by patients' ability to cope lies either in replacing the utility factor in the QALY model by a broader concept or in adding an objective functioning argument to the present model. As long as this has not been done, it is subjective utility that needs to be operationalized. As I have tried to show, this is better done by eliciting patients' self-reports than by eliciting hypothetical valuations. It seems to me that this is a major problem with most current operationalizations of QALYs.

5.2.4 *The Conventional Use of Hypothetical Valuations May Be Due to a Conflation of Issues*

Considering the various arguments, I find the controversy over whom to ask about health-related quality of life somewhat puzzling. Perhaps part of the explanation lies in a conflation of two issues. One is the measurement of quality of life associated with different health problems. The other is the measurement of distributive preferences in resource allocation. When QALYs are thought of as a measure of societal value – as has often been the case historically – health-state values have direct implications for resource allocation across diagnostic groups. The case for eliciting such values from the general population then becomes strong, since they are all potential patients with an interest in how resources are distributed. The problem looks different, however, if it is accepted that QALYs are one thing, societal value another. In societal valuation of a health program, a quality of life gain of a given size may receive different weighting depending on characteristics of the patients who receive it.

One can then envisage a two-step procedure for constructing a societal value model (Nord et al. 1999). The first step consists in measuring the severity of different health states. On the basis of such measurements, the quality of life gains associated with different health interventions may be estimated. The second step is to assign weights to different quality of life gains, taking into account, for instance, societal concerns for the severity of the patients' initial condition, the patients' potential for health, their age, or whatever other factors the public might consider to be of importance in an overall judgement of societal value. This second step is essentially about measuring distributive preferences. As noted above, there is a strong case for eliciting these from the general public. It is also possible to achieve the first step (quality of life measurement) by asking members of the general public to evaluate hypothetical health states. But with the separation of quality of life measurement from the measurement of distributive preferences, the case for asking the general population to judge the disutility of illness weakens. Prima facie, patients and the disabled are better judges of the burdens of their conditions than are healthy people.

5.3 HOW TO ASK

Assuming that we wish to ask patients (or disabled people) about the utility they experience with their condition, how should we ask them?

As noted earlier, three techniques are in use: the standard gamble, the time trade-off, and the rating scale. They are not equivalent. In most studies the first two have given significantly higher values than the last, and the standard gamble also tends to give higher values than the time trade-off (Nord 1992a). Economic evaluations in terms of QALYs that differ with respect to the way in which utilities were elicited are therefore not comparable. This is naturally a serious problem for potential users of economic evaluations.

There are a number of criteria by which the appropriateness of these techniques have been examined in the literature (Froberg and Kane 1989). These include grounding in theory, construct validity, convergent validity, test-retest reliability, and ease of use. So far these examinations have not led to the elimination of any of the techniques. A common attitude is that each of the techniques has its advantages and disadvantages, and that there is no clear winner (Torrance 1986; Williams 1988a; Gold et al. 1996). Exceptions are Nord (1992a) and Richardson (1994), who have emphasized the need to ask questions that are (*a*) *understandable* and (*b*) *verifiable* as capturing respondents' trade-offs between quantity and quality of life at an interval level of measurement. Nord and Richardson concluded that the time trade-off and the person trade-off fulfill these requirements to a greater extent than the standard gamble and the rating scale.

In the following, I expand on these points. I shall argue that the need for measurement at an interval level clears a third of the field, insasmuch as it seems fatal to the use of the rating scale. The need for understandability and verifiability, on the other hand, suggests a preference for the time trade-off technique over the standard gamble. But it also implies a narrowing of the range of health care across which comparisons of programs in terms of utility can at all be regarded as meaningful.

5.3.1 *The Level of Measurement*

As noted earlier, in the QALY model utility gains are summed over years and across persons, irrespective of the size of the gains and the utility of the initial conditions of the persons involved. This implies that an improvement from, for instance, 0.2 to 0.4 effectively is assigned the same significance (weight) in the estimation of aggregate utility as a gain from, for instance, 0.6 to 0.8, and twice as high significance (weight) as a gain for instance, from 0.6 to 0.7. In other words, the utility scores are used as though the utility scale had equal interval scale (cardinal) properties. This can only be justified if in the first place the utility scores are elicited in ways that allow subjects to express their strength of desire for different states in cardinal terms.

Responses to questions about willingness to sacrifice life expectancy have this property. If, for instance, users of crutches are willing to give up 10 percent of their remaining life years in order to become healthy, while wheelchair users are willing to give up 20 percent, then we may say that the willingness to sacrifice in the latter group is twice that in the former group. Utility scores that simply are linear transformations of such responses then also have cardinal properties. In the example above, the disutility of wheelchair users may be said to be twice that of those using crutches. From this it follows that moving a wheelchair user to the state of using crutches yields the same utility gain as restoring a user of crutches to normal functioning. This again implies that the improvement in the quality of life may be assumed to be equally significant to the two individuals concerned. Similarly, a movement from, for instance, 0.2 to 0.5 may be assumed to be of the same significance as a movement from 0.6 to 0.9. In general, movements on the 0–1 utility scale may be assumed to have a significance to the individuals concerned that is directly proportional to the size (length) of the movement, irrespective of the point from which the movement starts (irrespective of the utility score of the initial condition).

The cardinal properties of scores on a rating scale are much less evident. To see this, say a subject locates a state A at 80 and a state B at 60 on a scale from zero to a hundred. Has the subject then said that the disutility of state B is twice as big as the disutility of state A? If yes, in what sense is it "twice as big"?

The only way to find out about this is to ask subjects how they actually think when scoring health states on a rating scale. I am aware of two studies in which this was done. Both focused on the EuroQol Instrument (The EuroQol Group 1990). This is an instrument for eliciting peoples' valuations of hypothetical health states on a visual analogue scale from 0 ("worst imaginable health state") to 100 ("best imaginable health state"). Subjects are instructed to indicate how good or bad different states would be "for a person like you" by locating the states on the scale.

The first study was conducted by myself in a convenience sample of sixty-seven doctors and bioengineers (Nord 1991). In step one, the subjects valued six to eight states (the number varied). In step two, each subject was presented with a visual analogue scale where the particular values that he/she had used for two of the states in step one were reproduced. The instructions given were: "In the first questionnaire you have ranked the states. But you have done more than that. You have also assigned each state a numerical value on a scale from 0 to 100. I have reproduced two of the states as well as the values you have assigned to them. You could have chosen other numbers without changing the rank ordering. My question is: Why did you choose precisely these numbers? In other words: What does it mean that you have assigned the value (. . .) to state A and the value (. . .) to state B? Please write down your personal interpretation of the numbers. (If you don't mean anything in particular by them, you may of course write that.)"

Nineteen out of sixty-seven subjects explained the numbers in terms of "percentages of the best imaginable state." These nineteen subjects were the only ones who used any kind of cardinal measurement term in their explanations. None of them made any reference to life-year weights, trade-offs, or willingness to sacrifice. Eleven other subjects (including nine doctors) explicitly stated that they did not mean anything in particular by the numbers or that the numbers were randomly chosen. The remaining thirty-seven respondents did not comment on the numbers at all. They merely pointed out which elements in each state they had emphasized or indicated in words how bad they considered the state to be.

The study was later replicated in a British study in a sample of forty-one students, with almost identical results. The majority either did not at all answer the question about meaning or reported that they did not mean anything in particular by the numbers they had assigned to different states. Eleven subjects explained their responses in terms of "percentages of fitness" (Morris and Durand 1989). Lack of meaning in health-state valuations using the rating scale is later noted also by Ubel et al. (1998).

Going back to our question above, the conclusion to be drawn from these studies is that if subjects assign the values of, for instance, 80 and 60 to two health states using the EuroQol rating scale, then we may *not* infer that the disutility of the latter state is viewed as twice as big as the disutility of the former. We can only conclude that it is viewed as bigger. This is the same as saying that it would be unjustified to use EuroQol rating scale values as utility scores in a QALY calculation unless one were able to demonstrate that they actually coincide with scores that do have cardinal properties.

The Quality of Well-Being Scale (QWB, Kaplan and Anderson 1988) is another instrument that asks subjects to value health states on a rating scale. The instrument has wide use in North America, and a version of it was used as a basis for calculating QALYs when the state of Oregon set up its first draft priority list in 1991 for procedures to be covered by the state's Medicaid scheme (Oregon Health Services Commission 1991). But the QWB does no more than the EuroQol Instrument to induce subjects to think in cardinal terms. The utility scores it produces are therefore just as devoid of cardinal meaning as EuroQol numbers (Nord 1993c).

In a seminal paper on utility measurement in health economics, Torrance (1986) is well aware of the above problem. He therefore stresses the need for researchers using a rating scale to make it clear to the subjects that the scale is supposed to have equal interval properties. Presumably this implies giving examples like "If you think the increase in quality of life associated with moving from state A to state B is twice the increase associated with moving from B to C, then you should locate these three states on the scale such that the distance from A to B is twice the distance from B to C." But people do not normally think or speak of quality of life in cardinal terms. So in what sense might one increase in health yield twice as much as another? An answer could be offered in terms of willingness to sacrifice. But the rating scale exercise by definition does not ask about that. And the studies mentioned above tell us that subjects do not think in such terms when responding either.

I conclude that there is no basis for interpreting valuations of health state on a rating scale at a cardinal level. It follows that they should not be used as inputs in QALY calculations.

5.3.2 Understandability and Verifiability

As noted above, responses to standard gamble and time trade-off questions have cardinal properties. They therefore pass the measurement level test that rating scale responses fail. The criterion I suggest as a basis for making a choice between the standard gamble and the time trade-off is a value judgment. My starting point is that numbers are for counting. So if someone produces a utility number, then he must have counted something. Now, broadly speaking, utility means sense of well-being. As noted above, this concept is normally not associated with numbers at all. It is therefore reasonable for a potential user of utility numbers to ask what it is that has been counted by the numbers. *The value judgment I make is that utility must be defined such as to (1) allow a response to this question that practical decision makers can understand at a conceptual level and (2) allow the decision makers in principle to verify that the count is correct.* This is very much in line with suggestions made by Richardson (1994).

I call this a value judgment because I believe that users of utility numbers should understand what they are doing. This is not trivial. Numbers have status and power due to their simplicity and seeming precision. Decision makers have a fascination with numbers and may be ready to use them even if they have not properly thought through their meaning. The obvious example here is the first draft priority list for Medicaid in the state of Oregon (Oregon Health Services Commission 1991). The constructors of the list used utility numbers from the Quality of Well-Being Scale (Kaplan and Anderson 1988) to estimate the societal value of various medical procedures. The numbers were in fact unfit for this purpose (Eddy 1991; Nord 1993c), and the result was a list that was quite unacceptable to the public (Hadorn 1991).

Given the propensity in decision makers to use those numbers which are available, I also believe that producers of utility numbers have a moral obligation to explain to potential users exactly what the numbers they bring to the marketplace mean and to do their best to prevent unjustified uses of the numbers. This is no different from what is demanded of producers of goods and services in general. But again it is a value judgment, with which everyone will not necessarily agree.

Having said this, I must add that understandability and verifiability may also be necessary conditions for application. Though many decision makers are fascinated by numbers, there certainly also are many who hesitate to use numbers they do not understand and/or cannot verify. This is reflected in the fact that, in spite of the large number of cost-effectiveness analyses that have been published in the last twenty years using QALYs as the measure of benefit, the instances of these analyses having influenced resource allocation decisions are few and far between (Ross 1994; Gold et al. 1996). So ensuring understandability and verifiability of utility numbers serves two purposes: to prevent unjustified use of the numbers, on the one hand, and to gain acceptance for a more widespread justified use of them, on the other.

How, then, is utility defined in economic literature? A number of definitions exist. In fact, the use of the term varies to such an extent that some health economists tend to avoid it (Richardson 1994). Here I shall focus on two interpretations. One is in terms of quantities of wellness; the other in terms of subjective assignment of value. To see the difference between these, consider the way in which QALYs are calculated for an individual with a utility score of, say, 0.8 and a life expectancy of, say, ten years (assuming, for simplicity, no time preference):

$$\text{QALYs} = 0.8 \times 10$$

One way of interpreting the number 0.8 is to say that it is a measure of the strength of the individual's inner feeling of wellness. The number of QALYs then represents this strength of sensation converted into a quantity of wellness experienced over time. I shall call this the "quantity of wellness interpretation."

Another way of interpreting the number 0.8 is to say that it expresses the value that the individual assigns to each year in the state in question relative to the value of a year in full health. The QALY number then expresses the number of years in full health that the individual regards as equally valuable as ten years in the state in question. I shall call this the "value interpretation."

The two interpretations focus on different kinds of psychological phenomena. Strength of inner feeling and experienced quantity of wellness are emotional categories. By contrast, the assignment of value is a more cognitive category. The point I want to make is that, while both the quantity-of-wellness interpretation and the value interpretation are conceptually meaningful, the verifiability of utility numbers may depend on the choice of basic interpretation, since they involve counting different kinds of psychological phenomena. This again has implications for the choice of technique for eliciting utilities, as these techniques – as we shall see shortly – conceptually are associated with different basic interpretations.

5.3.3 The Quantity-of-Wellness Interpretation of Utility

An individual's subjective, inner feelings cannot be directly observed. So how can a utility number be verifiable if it is defined in terms of strength of inner feeling? Similarly, how can a QALY estimate be verifiable if it refers to the quantity of wellness experienced by the individual?

Verification is possible to the extent that the inner feeling has an observable physical or behavioral correlate. The tighter the functional relationship between the inner feeling and the observable correlate, the more verifiable propositions about inner feelings in terms of utility numbers will be.

Expected utility theory (see, e.g., Schoemaker 1982) offers a simple answer to this quest for an observable correlate. According to the theory, alternative actions in health care are characterized by a set of possible outcomes and a set of probabilities corresponding to each outcome. The theory assumes that people, when offered a choice between different actions associated with such uncertainty of outcomes, choose the action with the greatest expected utility (in the "inner feeling" sense of the term). If this is true, then actions to which individuals are indifferent must yield the same expected utility. The utility of a health state, then, may be ascertained by observing preferences for actions with different sets of possible outcomes in a standard gamble exercise.

An example is as follows. A patient is in a state of illness A. He is given two options. One is to continue in state A with certainty. The other is to accept a lottery that will restore him to full health with a probability of p, but also involves a probability of 1-p that he will die immediately. A value p' is established at which the patient is indifferent between these two options. Given the assumption that the patient maximizes expected utility, the expected utility of the two options must be equal at this point of indifference. The expected utility of the certainty option is the utility of state A (U_A) times its probability – which is 1 – that is, U_A. If full health is assigned the utility of 1, and being dead the utility of 0, the expected utility of the lottery is $1 \times p' + 0 \times (1 - p)$, or p'. Hence, given the assumption that the patient aims at maximizing expected utility, the utility of health state A may be estimated as the probability p' at which the patient is indifferent between the certainty option and the lottery. The reported indifference probability p' is then the needed observable correlate to the goodness of the inner feeling associated with state A.

The question is: How tight is the relationship between the inner feeling and the reported indifference probability in practice? Or, in statistical terms: How much of the variance in p' is explained by variance in utility? In a sense this is impossible to answer, since utility itself cannot be observed.

One possible approach is an axiomatic one: that is, to assume that most people make rational choices on their own behalf, and that rationality by definition implies maximizing expected utility. Then the reported indifference probability p' is by definition a precise, linear function of the utility of the state in question. An alternative approach is to collect data that may cast light on the *plausibility* of the expected utility maximization hypothesis. There is a vast literature to this effect, but it is beyond the scope of this book to review this literature in detail. As an introduction, readers are referred to Shoemaker (1982). Suffice it to say here that, on the one hand, it tells us that p' is clearly correlated to a number of variables that one would assume are correlated to the inner feeling of wellness. This supports the use of p' as an *indicator* of utility. On the other hand, there is substantial research suggesting that p' is far from an ideal indicator. This research includes:

- evidence that people do not always seem to maximize expected outcomes when making choices under uncertainty with respect to goods other than health
- evidence that people have trouble judging the significance of differences between probabilities, particularly when the probabilities are either very small or very big. For instance, if a subject chooses $p' = 0.9$ for a state A and $p' = 0.99$ for state B, it is not clear that the subject considers the disutility of state A to be ten times that of state B.
- evidence that p' incorporates not only the feeling of wellness that subjects associate with a health state, but also their aversion to the risk of ending up in a worse state, particularly their aversion to risking death

To see the significance of this research, assume that two health states A and B have been assigned the scores 0.9 and 0.8 respectively on the basis of responses to standard gamble questions. Assume that a potential user asks what exactly these numbers mean empirically. Given the quantitative interpretation of the concept of utility, the producer of the number would have to respond, for instance, with examples of the following kind:

- For equal lengths of time, the quantity of wellness experienced by an average person in state A is 90 percent of that experienced in full health.

- Taking an average person from state B to state A yields the same increase in the quantity of wellness experienced by that person as taking him/her from state A to full health (for equal periods of time).
- Taking an average person from state B to full health for five years yields the same increase in the quantity of wellness experienced by this person as taking him/her to state A for ten years.

I appreciate that some researchers working in the field are quite comfortable with propositions in these terms. However, I also believe that many potential users will remain unconvinced by the propositions in the above examples due to a combination of three facts. First, the potential users are unable to observe the "quantities of wellness" associated with different health scenarios. Second, when direct observation of utility is replaced by posing standard gamble questions to the subjects, the ultimate targets of the measurement, that is, the inner feeling of wellness and the quantity of wellness over time, are not even mentioned. Instead the questions use other concepts like preference, indifference, and probability. Third, the indirect procedure (estimating utility by means of p') is empirically known to have both systematic and random errors (cf. the evidence listed above), the magnitude of which is difficult to judge.

What, then, about the time trade-off technique? Is that a more reliable observable correlate to subjects' inner feelings of wellness?

The time trade-off technique works as follows. A patient is in a state of illness A. He is given two options. Either he can live in this state for, say, ten years, or he can live in full health for a lesser number of years. He is then asked to indicate the (lesser) number of years in full health that he would consider equal in value to ten years in state A. If, for instance, this number is 8, and the value of a year in full health is 1, then it follows that he values each year in state A at 0.8.

In theory, it is possible to interpret the subjects' response in terms of quantities of wellness, that is, to assume that when he says that ten years in state A is equally valuable as eight years in full health, it is in the sense that the ten years in state A will allow him to experience as much wellness as the eight years in full health. Similarly, it is possible to interpret his valuation of each year in state A to mean that the intensity of his inner feeling of wellness in state A is 80 percent of the intensity of his feeling when in full health. However, the basis for such an interpretation is extremely tenuous.

First, unlike in the standard gamble case, there is no long-standing axiomatic theory in economics that claims that subjects aim at maximizing utility when responding to time trade-off questions. Second, there is the evidence, cited in the discussion of standard gamble, that people do not always seem to maximize expected outcomes when making choices with respect to goods other than health. This evidence bears on the interpretation of time trade-off responses as well. Third, it is a fact that subjects are not asked to think in terms of such concepts as strength of inner feeling or total quantity of wellness when responding to time trade-off questions. Fourth, there is general recognition that time trade-off responses are confounded by time preference (Gold et al. 1996). This is because the years of life that are sacrificed in the time trade-off come at the end of the given time span and, therefore, may be valued less because they are farther in the future.

In sum, it seems reasonable to say that time trade-off responses are not any more convincing than standard gamble responses as observable behavioral correlates to the inner feeling of wellness associated with health states. They are undoubtedly correlated with these feelings, but the *numbers* are no more than standard gamble responses verifiable as cardinal measurements of these feelings.

The overall conclusion I draw from this analysis is that the quantity-of-wellness interpretation of utility is understandable at the conceptual level. The problem is the verifiability of numbers that purport to count utility in this sense. Some claim that application of the standard gamble technique or the time trade-off technique resolves this problem. But counts made by means of these techniques are not verifiable empirically. In the case of the standard gamble, the numbers are verifiable axiomatically. However, this is not enough to satisfy the basic requirement for accepting a technique that I posited to start with.

It follows that the quantity-of-wellness interpretation of utilities and QALYs is a dead end. Instead we must look at the value interpretation, in the hope that utility numbers are more verifiable given this interpretation.

5.3.4 *The Value Interpretation of Utility*

As noted above, in the value interpretation a utility number expresses the value that the individual *assigns* to a year in a particular state relative to the value of a year in full health. The number of QALYs associated with, say, ten years in that state then expresses the number of years in full health that the individual regards as equally valuable as ten years in the state in question. So if 0.8 is the relative value assigned to the state, then ten years in this state are equivalent to eight healthy years, namely eight QALYs.

The standard gamble and the time trade-off may both be seen as techniques for measuring the assignment of value rather than as techniques for measuring feelings of well-being. But they assign value in different units of measurement. In other words, the utility numbers they produce are the results of counts of different phenomena. The question is: Which of these ways of counting is more understandable and verifiable to potential users?

Consider a state A that is assigned a utility of 0.8. If this number derives from a standard gamble exercise, it means that a year in state A is assigned the same value as being given an 80 percent chance of a whole year in full health and a 20 percent risk of dying at the beginning of the year. This number is verifiable: One needs simply to ask subjects, "Which do you prefer, an additional year in state A or an 80 percent chance of an additional year in full health combined with a 20 percent risk of dying at the beginning of the year?" If the subjects on average are indifferent, then the utility number is correct. If they are not indifferent, the utility number is wrong.

If, on the other hand, the number 0.8 derives from a time trade-off excercise, it means that a year in state A with certainty is assigned the same value as 0.8 years in full health with certainty. Again the number is verifiable. One need simply ask the subjects, "Which do you prefer, an additional year in state A or an additional 0.8 years in full health?" If the subjects on average are indifferent, then the number is correct. If they are not indifferent, the number is wrong. So, in terms of verifiability, the standard gamble and the time trade-off perform equally well within the value interpretation of utilities.

What, then, about understandability? To judge this, let us see how the researcher would have to answer if he were asked the following by a curious potential user: "When you assign a numerical value of 0.8 to state A, I assume that you have *counted* some phenomenon associated with this state. Which phenomenon is that?"

With the time trade-off the researcher would answer that he has counted the *time in full health* considered equivalent to a year in state A (and expressed this time as a proportion of a whole year). In short, a year in state A is as valuable as 0.8 healthy years.

With the standard gamble, the researcher would answer something like the following: The number 0.8 represents the lowest probability of survival that subjects would accept in a gamble that is supposed to be equivalent to living one year in state A with certainty and that has as its two possible outcomes one year in full health and immediate death. In terms of counting, the number 0.8 corresponds to *the proportion of people who would survive* if a large number of people accepted the gamble in question at the required survival probability.

It seems to me that the former of these explanations – concerning the TTO – is fairly straightforward. It is short, and it is understandable inasmuch as people are used to thinking of time as something we count.

By contrast, the latter explanation – concerning the standard gamble – is quite complicated. Even for a trained mind, it takes some concentration to grasp what the utility number corresponds to in the real world.

All else being equal, it would seem reasonable to conclude that the understandability of time trade-off based utilities is so much greater than standard gamble based ones that the time trade-off should be the preferred valuation technique.

5.3.5 Does the Standard Gamble Capture All Aversion to Risk?

Some will object that the above comparison is unfair. The standard gamble is necessarily more complicated than the time trade-off, because it addresses actions with uncertain outcomes, which are inherently more complicated to describe than actions the outcomes of which are certain. So if in fact the utility numbers are to be used to evaluate actions with uncertain outcomes – and this is more often than not the case with medical procedures – then we may have to live with the complexity of the standard gamble.

When judging this argument, we should bear in mind the assumption made earlier that the utilities we want to put into QALY calculations are ex post utilities. Now, consider a life-saving procedure that will bring an individual to state A with a probability of 0.8 and to state B with a probability of 0.2. So the expected utility of the procedure is:

$$E(U) = U_A \times 0.8 + U_B \times 0.2 \qquad (3)$$

where U_A and U_B are the ex post utilities of states A and B, respectively.

The expected utility in the equation above is simply the sum of the two possible ex post utilities weighted by their probabilities. This is not the same as the value of the procedure to the individual. Say U_A = 0.9 and U_B = 0.3. The expected utility is then 0.78. Ex ante the individual might be indifferent between this procedure and a procedure that with certainty would take him to a state with a utility of 0.60, on the basis that he dislikes risk. In other words, he may prefer to play it safe at a sufficing level rather than to maximize expected ex post utility at the expense of risking ending up with a utility of 0.3. In fact, there is empirical evidence that this is a normal attitude to medical treatment (Kahneman and Tversky 1983).

Now, assume that the utilities of A (0.9) and B (0.3) have been established ex post by means of the time trade-off. To calculate the ex ante value to the individuals of the procedure in question, the expected ex post utility (E(U)in equation [3] above) would have to be discounted by a factor reflecting the above-mentioned aversion to risk. In a calculation of the societal value of a proposed health-care program in terms of QALYs gained, this discounted expected utility would be the appropriate number to use.

Advocates of the standard gamble claim that such discounting for risk is unnecessary if the ex post utilities are based on standard gamble responses, since this technique allows subjects to take risk into account. To see that there is some truth in this, consider the typical standard gamble exercise that uses full health and immediate death as possible outcomes of the gamble. Assume that a state A scores 0.85 on the time trade-off and 0.95 on the standard gamble, and that the reason for this difference is that the time trade-off measures ex post utility only, while the standard gamble also encapsulates aversion to the risk of dying. Assume that we wish to evaluate a treatment for people in state A with a life expectancy of, say, ten years. The treatment has as its possible outcomes full health with a probability of 0.9 and a life expectancy of ten years, and immediate death with a probability of 0.1. Then the expected ex post utility of the state people will be in after intervention is 0.90. This is higher than the time trade-off based ex post utility of state A (0.85). A time trade-off based QALY calculation would therefore suggest that these people would prefer the intervention to staying in state A. In *reality* they might not have this preference, because of their aversion to the risk of dying. This would be neatly captured if the standard gamble score for state A were used in the utility assessment rather than the time trade-off score. The expected utility of the state after intervention would then be *lower* than the utility of state A (0.90 versus 0.95), suggesting that staying in state A would be preferable to having the intervention.

However, as explained originally by Richardson (1994), the standard gamble captures aversion to risk in the specific context in which the standard gamble utilities are elicited. It does not follow that these utilities capture the strength of risk aversion in other contexts.

To see this, let us return to our previous example of a life-saving procedure that will take people to one of two states A and B (Equation [3] above). Assume that the utilities for states A and B have been estimated as 0.95 and 0.4 respectively by means of standard gamble questions using full health and immediate death as possible outcomes of the gamble. These scores reflect not only the ex post utility associated with these states, but also the subjects' aversion to the risk of dying. This aversion drives the choice of indifference level for the survival probability in the gamble upward on the 0–1 scale. In other words, the estimates for U_A and U_B based on standard gamble will be higher than the true ex post utilities. The calculation of expected utility based on these estimates will then also be higher than the true expected ex post utility. So the use of the standard gamble in the initial valuation of states A and B does *not* accommodate the need to discount expected ex post utility in a societal ex ante valuation of this particular risky intervention. On the contrary, it leads to a higher valuation result than the pure calculation of expected ex post utility would do.

The example shows that the need to discount for risk aversion in ex ante evaluations of health-care interventions cannot be met by incorporating risk aversion into the utility assessments themselves. Discounting for risk should be included in the societal value function as an argument in addition to ex post utilities.

I therefore reject the complaint that it is not fair to compare the standard gamble and the time trade-off in terms of their understandability. They must both be judged as techniques for eliciting ex post utilities. Here I come back to my conclusion above. With both techniques, respondents may be seen as assigning values to health states (as opposed to expressing feelings of wellness), and both techniques yield verifiable numbers. But time trade-off utilities have a much simpler empirical interpretation, and therefore are far easier to understand, than standard gamble utilities.

5.3.6 *Evidence-Based, Understandable, and Verifiable Utilities*

What I have said so far, may be summarized in five points:

1. QALY calculations purport to capture what actually comes out of different health interventions. Utilities for use in QALY calculations should therefore be measured ex post. Aversion to risk and time preference need to be incorporated into the societal value function in terms of separate discount factors.
2. Ex post utilities should be based on patients' (or former patients') self-reports rather than on people's valuation of hypothetical health states with which they have limited direct experience.
3. It is not sufficient to elicit utilities by means of rating scales, because responses on such scales do not have the necessary cardinal scale properties.
4. To be understandable and verifiable, utility numbers need to be interpreted as values assigned to life years in different states rather than measures of feelings of wellness.
5. Given this interpretation, both the standard gamble and the time trade-off yield verifiable numbers. But time trade-off utilities are preferable to standard gamble utilities, because they have a much simpler empirical interpretation, and therefore are far easier to understand.

So when a curious potential user of utility numbers asks what a utility number U for a health state A actually stands for, I suggest that the researcher answer that it is the proportion of a year in full health considered as valuable as a full year in state A, judged ex post by a person in state A. By choosing this interpretation and the measurement procedures that go with it, the researcher may ensure that the utility number is evidence-based, understandable, and verifiable.

This is the good news. The bad news is that, given this interpretation of utility numbers, there are two classes of health interventions the societal value of which seems difficult to capture in the QALY approach. These are, on the one hand, services that lead to minor functional improvements, and, on the other hand, life-saving procedures – in other words, services at the two extreme ends of a societal value continuum for health services. Let us look at each of these limitations in turn.

5.3.7 *The Utility of Minor and Moderate Improvements*

When the utility of a condition is operationally defined as the proportion of a year in full health that is judged equivalent to a full year in the condition, then the *disutility* of the condition (one minus the utility) expresses the subject's willingness to give up life time to be cured of the condition. The underlying assumption is then that willingness to sacrifice life time in order to get well is proportional to the disutility of the health state. It is important to realize that this relationship between disutility and willingness to sacrifice is not a logical truism. Feelings of disutility on the one hand, and willingness to sacrifice on the other, are separate psychological phenomena, which need not be functionally related in any simple way. Only empirical studies can tell us what the relationship really is.

One reason to doubt that the relationship is one of simple proportionality is that life time is a complex good involving all arenas of life and therefore is associated with extremely high value. Some people may always prefer to endure the disutility of ill health rather than to give up life time in order to be spared health-related disutility. Others may be willing to sacrifice life time only if it is to obtain substantial increases in utility in return. While undeniably valuable, minor and moderate increases in health may not be valuable enough to justify sacrificing all the nonhealth-related kinds of utility that life time has to offer.

What, then, does the evidence tell us?

One piece of evidence has been cited earlier, namely the study of Sherbourne et al. (1997). They collected time trade-off and standard gamble data from close to 18,000 patients visiting primary care clinics in fifty locations across the United States. On average, the patients had two chronic conditions. Their average score on a rating scale from 0 ("worst possible health state") to 100 ("perfect health") was 75. However, 70 percent of the patients were not willing to sacrifice any life expectancy in order to be relieved of their condition.

Other smaller studies accord with that of Sherbourne et al. O'Leary et al. (1995) studied a sample of 124 cancer patients with a median rating scale score of 0.75 and an interquartile range of 0.58 to 0.85. Seventeen of these patients were not willing to sacrifice any life expectancy (as measured in a time trade-off exercise) to exchange their current condition for "excellent health." Of these seventeen, fifteen had scored themselves below unity on the rating scale. The median rating scale score in these seventeen patients was 0.84. O'Leary et al. suggested that there might be a threshold level for health states above which patients were not willing to sacrifice any life expectancy in order to get well.

Fowler et al. (1995) interviewed 291 patients with AIDS. They asked the patients about their desire to be resuscitated "if their heart stopped today," assuming that variability across patients with respect to such a desire could in part be explained by differences in current health status. However, they also assumed that variability in the desire for resuscitation could be explained by differences in more basic attitudes to the value of life. They assessed such differences by means of a question about the patients' desire for life-extending efforts were they to find themselves in undesirable states like being chronically nauseated or blind. The authors found that the desire to be resuscitated "if their heart stopped today" had little to do with the patients' current health status. It was mostly explained by their general reluctance to relinquish life, as expressed in their desire for life-extending measures in given, undesirable conditions. Fowler et al. conclude that "these data make it very likely that standard gamble and time trade-off questions confound the value of health status with 'a reluctance to give up life.' For this reason, if measuring how people value a health state is the goal, they are likely not to be the right measures to use" (p. 199).

In a survey done in Norway of quality of life in patients with long-standing illnesses, including diabetes, arthritis, osteoporosis, psoriasis, and lower-back pain, 75 out of 230 patients were not willing to sacrifice any life time in order instead to live as healthy. Forty-seven of these 75 nonetheless reported that their health problems had affected their mood and quality of life in the past year (29 a little, 9 moderately, 5 a good deal, 4 very much; preliminary results reported in Nord 1996b).

These studies support the hypothesis that there is no simple linear relationship between feelings of disutility resulting from illness and the willingness to sacrifice life expectancy to be relieved of illness. They suggest that, in people with moderate health problems, time trade-off questions are not sensitive enough to pick up real and significant losses of quality of life. If, then, time trade-off measurements in patients are used to calculate QALYs, the value of relieving people of moderate problems will be estimated as being very small or even nil, since their pretreatment time trade-off scores on the 0–1 utility scale will be unity or very close to unity. This in all probability is a poor representation of actual societal values.

This sensitivity problem could be taken as an argument in favor of using other techniques for valuing health states than the time trade-off technique – for instance, the standard gamble or the rating scale of even willingness to pay. The two latter candidates are certainly more sensitive techniques. I nonetheless dismiss them here, since I have already laid down the premise that the disutility of a condition in the QALY approach needs to be defined as the individual's willingness to give up life expectancy to be cured of the condition. Subjects do not have this issue in mind when valuing health by means of rating scales or willingness-to-pay questions.

With respect to the standard gamble, I am not aware of evidence suggesting that this technique is more sensitive than the time trade-off when used to elicit self-ratings in patients. On the contrary, the study by Sherbourne et al. (1997) referred to above does not suggest that this is the case. This is not surprising. It seems reasonable that people who are reluctant to give up life in terms of distant years to gain moderate health improvements are also reluctant to risk their lives at present for the same purpose. Also, as noted earlier, indifference probabilities close to unity in standard gamble exercises cannot be interpreted as having a cardinal meaning. So even if the standard gamble should produce numbers slightly less than 1 for moderate conditions that score 1 on the time trade-off, it would be difficult to justify use of such numbers as utilities in QALY calculations.

The problem with lack of sensitivity to the disutility of minor ailments could also be resolved if one used ex ante judgments of the utility of health states exercised by samples of the general population instead of judgments by patients ex post. For instance, in the ex ante approach, time trade-off scores in the order of 0.8–0.85 have been reported for states like "some problems with walking about" and "moderate pain" (Williams 1995b). But again, sensitivity is of little use if the numbers do not have the meaning we want them to have. The effect of substituting ex ante judgments for ex post judgments would be fundamentally to change the QALY concept from an evidence-based outcome measure to a measure based on beliefs. It would be a pseudosolution to a real problem.

The conclusion I reach is that when we choose a way of defining and measuring utility that makes utility numbers evidence-based, understandable, and verifiable, we do that at the price of restricting the range of services for which QALY calculations may be valid to services with relatively large effects on patients' functioning. That is a major problem. I now address another one.

5.3.8 *The Ex Ante Value of Life-Saving Procedures*

Consider the following two outcomes:

A. Taking a person with a TTO-based utility score of 0.9 and a life expectancy of forty years to full health, with the same life expectancy. Since forty years at 0.9 is equal to thirty-six years in full health, the gain is equivalent to obtaining four healthy years on top of thirty-six healthy years.
B. Saving a person's life and giving him twenty years in full health.

Given the interpretation of utility suggested above, the ex post utility of these two outcomes may meaningfully be compared in cardinal terms: Outcome A is equivalent to providing four healthy years, while outcome B is twenty healthy years. So the ex post utility of A (the value assigned to A by the recipient) is one-fifth of the ex post utility of B (the value assigned to B by its recipient).

In resource allocation decisions, these two outcomes would be compared *ex ante*. In the QALY approach, they would then be compared in terms of the *ex ante value to the individuals concerned*, where the ex ante value is a product of the ex post utility and discount factors for time preference and risk aversion (see equation [2] earlier in this chapter). The question I want to raise here is whether this would be feasible at the cardinal level that the QALY approach presupposes.

A first attempt could be to say that, since the four gained years to which outcome A is equivalent on average come later than the twenty gained years of outcome B, the ex ante value of outcome A to the individual concerned is less than one-fifth of the ex ante value of outcome B. The *exact* ex ante value of outcome A relative to outcome B may be calculated by discounting at some annual rate the ex post utilities of all gained years in A and B to their corresponding present (ex ante) value. Since the gained years in outcome A on average are more distant than the gained years in outcome B, the discounting will reduce the value of outcome A relatively more than it will reduce the value of outcome B. The result of the discounting will then, for instance, be that the ex ante value of A is one-tenth of the ex ante value of B.

However, how can the latter proposition be verified? The only way to do so is to observe whether the individuals concerned ex ante really value outcome B ten times as much as outcome A. How can one observe that?

A first problem is that is impossible to observe subjects' direct choices between these two outcomes, since the two outcomes presuppose different initial positions. In one, the individual has a life expectancy (without intervention) of zero, while in the other he has a life expectancy of forty years. The individual cannot possibly be in both these positions at the same time.

A number of ways around this problem might be tried. First, one could ask people to imagine themselves in these two situations and to express their hypothetical willingness to sacrifice in order to obtain the outcomes in question. Second, one could assume that different individuals value different kinds of health benefits in much the same way. Under this assumption one could compare one group of individuals' willingness to sacrifice in order to obtain outcome A with another group's willingness to sacrifice to have their lives saved. While these two approaches could not be in terms of willingness to sacrifice probability of survival (the standard gamble) or expected life years (the time trade-off), as people on the verge of dying possess none of these goods, the willingness to sacrifice could be measured in terms of, for instance, willingness to pay. Third, one could ask people to value health improvements relative to small reductions in the risk of imminent death and then calculate the value of avoiding certain death by "multiplying up."

However, all of these approaches assume that people's willingness to sacrifice goods in their own life in order to have their life saved can be expressed in finite terms. Is this plausible? Goods have no value to oneself if life itself is lost. Facing immediate death due to illness (as opposed to old age) is also an absolutely devastating situation. The continuation of life itself would seem priceless to the individual concerned. It seems difficult then to obtain individual ex ante valuations of outcome B above in meaningful, finite terms. In general this means that, while it is possible to speak meaningfully of the *ex post utility* of life-saving procedures relative to health-improving ones, it seems difficult to compare the two in terms of individuals' assignments of *ex ante values*, as the QALY approach presupposes.

5.3.9 *Summary and Conclusion*

Let me summarize again. I have tried to define and operationalize QALYs in such a way as to make them evidence-based, understandable, and verifiable. A first step was to define utility as the value *assigned* to a health state, measured as the proportion of a year in full health that is equivalent to a full year in the state as judged ex post by people in that state. Second, the product of a utility number U for a state A, and a number of years N, is interpreted as the value of being in state A for N years, measured as an equivalent number of healthy years, again judged ex post by people in state A. Third, multiplying the ex post value of a scenario consisting of being in state A for N years (expressed as an equivalent number of healthy years) by a discount factor for distance in time yields the number of QALYs associated with the scenario. This is interpreted as the value assigned ex ante to such a scenario by informed individuals who are offered it as an outcome for themselves.

The points I have made in the two preceding sections refer to this evidence-based, understandable, and verifiable version of the QALY approach. The first point is that the utility assigned to light or moderate states of illness tend to be the same as the utility assigned to full health. The societal value of curing people with such conditions then tends to be nil. This is not because that is how society really feels, but rather because of the *lack of sensitivity* in the only technique for eliciting utilities that makes utility numbers fully evidence-based, understandable, and verifiable. The second point is that the ex ante value assigned by patients to life-saving procedures tends to be infinite and therefore is difficult to express as a finite QALY number that may be compared with the number of QALYs provided, for instance, by health-improving interventions.

In short, if the QALY approach to estimating the societal value of health-care interventions is operationalized such as to make it evidence-based, understandable, and verifiable, then it does not seem to work for outcomes at the upper and lower ends of the societal value continuum for health-care services. This is a serious problem, given the fact that a main virtue of the QALY approach has always been its alleged capacity to cover the whole range of health-care services.

The problem is due to the basic assumption in the QALY approach that societal value is the sum of individual valuations. Individuals may certainly, in some circumstances, be prepared to make a trade-off between quality of life and life itself, but not easily so at the two ends of the health continuum that extends from a life-threatening condition to full health. In the next chapter I shall argue that, if we want to have a measure of societal value that captures both quality and length of life, we need to change our basic interpretation of values for health states and measure these by means of a technique that uses a societal perspective rather than an individual perspective.

Chapter 6

Ways to Go

6.1 THE PROBLEMS

Let me bring together the main points of the two previous chapters. The QALY approach, in its initial form, equates the societal value of a health-care intervention with the sum of individual utility gains produced by the activity. This has the following implications:

A. The societal value of an outcome in one individual is proportional to the size of the utility gain in that individual.
B. The societal value of utility gains of a given size are the same, irrespective of the severity of the patient's initial condition.
C. The societal value of an outcome in one individual is close to proportional to the duration of the utility gain.
D. From B it follows that the societal value of an outcome with life-long duration is inversely proportional to the patient's age.
E. Societal value is proportional to the number of people who get to enjoy a particular benefit.

Unfortunately, each of these propositions is contradicted by evidence. The assumption of utility maximization is simply not tenable, in neither the caring-for-others nor the self-interest perspective.

Some will argue that this could be remedied by constructing an alternative valuation model in which the functional relationship between individual utility gains and societal value is specified differently. For instance, one could add weights for severity of initial condition and for age, and discount factors for the duration of gains and for the number of people helped. Such a modified model could still be called a QALY model, inasmuch as individual utility gains would

113

still be the basic source of societal value, only at a transformation rate different from that presumed in the conventional QALY model.

There are two problems with this. One is that the data for estimating the parameters of such an alternative model are simply not available at present. In particular, we do not know enough to estimate even roughly the quantitative relationship between societal value on the one hand and patients' age, the duration of benefits and the number of people helped on the other. A quantitative model that includes parameters for these factors will therefore at present be highly arbitrary and difficult to justify.

This, of course, need not be more than a temporary problem. It is presumably only a matter of time before researchers have collected much more data on the relationships between societal value and such factors as patients' age, the duration of benefits, and the number of people helped. In the meantime, to avoid arbitrariness, one could construct a model that includes parameters only for those factors for which reasonably valid data are available. For instance, one could estimate the "severity weighted utility gain" (SWUG!) of different interventions. This would consist in multiplying the utility gain of an intervention – as measured on the conventional 0–1 scale – by a factor reflecting societal concerns for the severity of the condition before intervention, as shown in the last section of Chapter 4. Estimates of benefits in terms of "SWUGs" could then be used to compare the cost-effectiveness of health-care projects that on the one hand, are similar with respect to patients' age and the number of years that patients get to enjoy benefits (factors the importance of which we do not know enough about), but, on the other hand, differ with respect to severity and utility gains.

But then we run into the second problem. As shown in Chapter 5, the measurement of health gains in terms of individual utility gains works in only a limited part of the range of possible outcomes of health care. In terms of "SWUGs," the societal value of moderate health improvements would tend to be nil, and the value of life-saving procedures would tend to be infinitely high. None of these evaluations would be consistent with real societal preferences for resource allocation.

In sum, then, in contrast to the original ambitions of the QALY approach, a modified, evidence-based and utility-based valuation model would be usable for making comparisons across a somewhat limited number of health-care services.

Is it, then, impossible to value all different kinds of health outcomes on a common cardinal scale in an evidence-based, verifiable, and understandable way? Have the visions of health economists during the last twenty-five years been too optimistic? Is cost-effectiveness analysis doomed to be used in only selected areas of health care, in which it is meaningful and feasible to measure outcomes by such techniques as the standard gamble and the time trade-off?

Not necessarily. But I believe that to construct a more fully usable measure of value in health care, one needs to focus more strongly on and adhere more strictly to the purpose of such values in informing resource allocation decisions.

6.2 THE PERSON TRADE-OFF ISSUE REVISITED

As noted in Chapter 1, the purpose of assigning numerical values to health outcomes is to establish the trade-offs that society wishes to make between competing programs or projects that – due to differences with respect to costs per person treated – include different numbers of patients. The purpose, in other words, is to establish person trade-offs on the value side that are comparable to person trade-offs on the production side (the latter showing up in the cost data). To establish such person trade-offs is essentially also the ambition of the QALY model. However, it seems to me that in choosing this particular approach, health economists have made things both too easy and too difficult for themselves. First, they have chosen to say that the person trade-off on the value side is determined by the amount of individual utility produced by given interventions. This is too easy, in the sense that it is simply an assumption based on researchers' own intuition rather than on systematic observation of societal values. Second, the assumption invokes a concept the meaning of which is far from clear, namely that of the utility to individuals of being in different health states, measured at a cardinal level. This is an unnecessary complication. What ultimately is needed in resource allocation decisions is not utilities for health states per se, but rather societal values for different health improvements relative to each other (including life saving). The QALY approach uses utilities for health states to establish societal values for improvements in health by defining the latter as differentials between health-state utilities. *But there is no need for utilities for health states in informing resource allocation decisions if society's valuation of different improvements in health can be mea-*

sured directly. Fortunately, this is not only possible but has in fact already been done in many studies.

Let us use the term "direct outcome valuation" for the direct societal valuation of different health improvements relative to each other. Since, in a resource allocation context, the purpose of outcome valuation is to establish person trade-offs on the value side, the intuitively natural valuation technique is to ask direct person trade-off questions. The framing of such questions is described in Chapter 4. Essentially, the researcher specifies the characteristics of outcomes of different kinds and asks representative samples of society to express the number of people obtaining one kind of outcome that would be regarded as equivalent to a given number of people obtaining another kind of outcome.

The main advantage of direct-outcome valuation in terms of person trade-offs is that it avoids the problems associated with utility measurement at the upper and lower ends of the value continuum of health interventions. Consider first the valuation of a moderate improvement in health, for instance, curing a person who has considerable problems walking about and moderate pain part of the day. As we have seen, evidence suggests that many people in conditions of this degree of severity or less are not prepared to sacrifice any life expectancy in order to get cured. On the other hand, ample evidence suggests that society not only values such cures but is prepared to make person trade-offs between such cures and treatments for more serious conditions. In other words, while the individual utility approach is too insensitive to establish person trade-offs for moderate or slight health improvements, direct person trade-off questions do produce meaningful numerical responses for such improvements.

Consider, second, the valuation of life-saving interventions. In terms of individual utility the valuation will tend to be infinite. But in terms of societal person trade-offs it is not. Societies are all the time setting limits to the amount of resources they want to spend on costly life-saving interventions for the few, in order to have sufficient resources to spend on interventions that offer significant improvements in health to larger numbers of people. Indeed, this was the start of the Oregon prioritization experiment. It also comes out in responses to hypothetical person trade-off questions (see Chapter 4). In effect, this is to assign a finite societal value to life-saving interventions.

In short, compared to the individual utility questions used in the QALY approach, direct person trade-off questions allow analysts to value a broader range of health outcomes. As I have said, I regard this as the main advantage of the person trade-off approach. But this is not the only advantage. As noted in Chapter 4, the person trade-off approach also allows encapsulation of concerns for fairness. Suffice it here to reiterate the two aspects of fairness discussed in Chapter 4 that are particularly salient in societal value judgments in health care and that run counter to the maximization of QALYs. First, there is the widely held view that patients have stronger claims to treatment the more severely ill they are. The strength with which this view is held shows up numerically when subjects are asked to express person trade-offs between programs for patients in conditions of differing degrees of severity. Second, there is the view that patients have much the same right to realize their potential for health whether this potential is large or only modest. Also, this view shows up when subjects are asked to express person trade-offs between programs for equally ill patients with different potentials for improvement. As shown in Chapter 4, these concerns for fairness, elicited by means of the person trade-off technique, can be encapsulated in values for health states by adhering to the following rules of thumb:

Dead: 0.00

Severe problem (e.g., a person who sits in a wheelchair, has pain most of the time, and is unable to work): 0.65–0.85

Considerable problem (e.g., a person who uses crutches for walking, has light pain intermittently and is unable to work): 0.90–0.94

Moderate problem (e.g., a person who has difficulty moving about outdoors and has slight discomfort, but is able to do some work and has only minor difficulties at home): 0.98–0.995

Healthy: 1.00

It is important to note that these numbers *are not utilities.* They are simply a way of representing, in a compact implicit way, societal preferences for resource allocation in terms of person trade-offs. The *differences in value* between the different levels reflect these person trade-offs. The numbers encapsulate three aspects of fairness. First, life-saving interventions will in general receive much higher valuations in an economic analysis than health-improving ones. For instance, a program that is expected to restore 10 people from dying to a healthy life will be valued as highly as a program that is expected to cure 100–150 people with a "considerable problem," as exemplified above. Second, improvements for the severely ill will tend to receive much higher valuations than improvements for the moderately ill. For instance, a program that is expected to cure 10 people at the "severe problem" level will be valued as highly as a program that is expected to cure on the order of 250 people at the "moderate problem" level. Third, there will be only modest differences between the valuations of improvements for equally ill patients with differences in potential for improvement. For instance, a program that is expected to cure 10 people of a severe problem will be valued only marginally more than a program that is expected to take another group of 10 people from the "severe" level to the "moderate" level.

After the values in the Rules of Thumb were published (Nord, 1996a), a more comprehensive set of values was established for use in economic evaluation of health care in Norway. The set uses a scale of severity of illness as shown in Table 13.

The scale derives from a scale initially constructed by Sintonen (1981). Modifications were made to achieve a scale in which the different intervals, to the extent possible, would be perceived as representing equally big increases in terms of quality of life (Nord 1993a). Using some Norwegian person trade-off data in addition to those referred to in Chapter 4, values were assigned to the different levels on the severity scale as shown in Table 14 (Nord 1996c; Nord et al. 1999).

6.3 ACKNOWLEDGING THE VALUE OF DISABLED PEOPLE'S LIVES

One of the main equity issues addressed in this book is the concern for allowing people to realize their potential for health, whether this is large or small. The concept of differences in potential has two somewhat different aspects. If two patients A and B are equally ill, and health care can improve functioning more in A than in B, then A has a greater potential for health than B. This is the way I have used the concept of potential hitherto. I suggest that society wishes to strike a balance between producing as great functional improvements as possible and helping each individual realize his or her highest possible level of functioning. One purpose of letting health-state values have strong upper-end compression is to encapsulate this *balanced* view regarding functional improvements in people with non-life-threatening conditions.

However, variation in potential is also an issue in the valuation of

Table 13. *A scale of severity of illness*

Level	Examples
1. Healthy	
2. Slight problem	Can move about anywhere but has difficulties walking more than a kilometer
3. Moderate problem	Can move about without difficulties at home but has difficulties on stairs and outdoors
4. Considerable problem	Moves about with difficulty at home; needs assistance on stairs and outdoors
5. Severe problem	Can sit. Needs help to move about – both at home and outdoors
6. Very severe problem	To some degree bedridden; can sit in a chair part of the day if helped by others
7. Completely disabled	Permanently bedridden
8. Dead	

Table 14. *Values for different levels of severity of illness*

Severity level	Value
1. Healthy	1.00
2. Slight problem	0.9999
3. Moderate problem	0.99
4. Considerable problem	0.92
5. Severe problem	0.80
6. Very severe problem	0.65
7. Completely disabled	0.40
8. Dead	0.00

life-extending interventions for people with different permanent levels of functioning. The permanently disabled have, by definition, a lower potential for health than the healthy. If the logic of conventional QALY analysis is directly translated into policy, life years gained by disabled people will be regarded as less valuable than life years gained by healthy people. As noted above, the upper-end compression of health states as in seen Table 14 eliminates much of this devaluation of life-extending programs for the disabled. However, with life-extending programs, people may not want to strike a *balance* between health maximization and realization of individual potentials. Rather, I suspect they want the healthy and the disabled to be treated *on com-*

pletely equal terms, on the ground that people's interest in and entitlement to continued life is largely independent of their state of health (Harris 1987; Nord 1993d; see also the public and political reactions to the first cost-per-QALY-based priority list in the state of Oregon, U.S.A.).

If this is correct, it calls for yet another refinement of the conventional QALY model in assessments of societal value. Fortunately, this is not difficult to achieve technically. A preference for nondiscrimination in matters of life saving may be encapsulated in QALY calculations simply by saying that *for all health states that are preferred to death, all saved life years count as one* (Nord et al. 1999; Ubel et al. in press). Values for health states, as for instance in Table 14, should then not be interpreted as values of life itself for people at different levels of functioning. The values will not apply to life-extending procedures for the chronically ill or the disabled. They will only be relevant in estimating the value of different *improvements in symptoms and functioning* for people with nonfatal conditions, relative to each other and relative to the prevention of premature death.

Some may find it illogical that there should not be a devaluation of additional life years provided to people with illness when most people do seem to be willing to make a trade-off between length of life and quality of life when asked standard gamble and time trade-off questions. I do not see a problem with this, for two reasons. First, individuals' real willingness to trade off their own life expectancy for quality of life is probably not as widespread as is suggested by preference studies in healthy people who are asked to imagine themselves in states of illness. As noted earlier, when standard gamble or time trade-off questions are asked of real patients, people with moderate illness or disability tend to be unwilling to sacrifice life expectancy to become healthy. Second, one cannot always expect consistency across decision contexts. The fact that an individual says that he personally would be willing to sacrifice years at the end of life, or chances of survival in order to gain quality of life, does not necessarily mean that he supports a public policy that discriminates between the healthy and the disabled in the provision of reliable life-extending procedures.

Altogether, I believe that restricting the use of health-state values less than 1 to health-improving programs is a simple and valid way to eliminate a discriminatory effect of the conventional QALY model that upper-end compression of health states does not fully prevent.

6.4 DISABILITY-ADJUSTED LIFE YEARS (DALYS)

As noted in the Introduction, the World Health Organization is organizing a large international collaborative enterprise called the *Global Burden of Disease (GBD) Project* (Murray and Lopez 1996). The idea behind the project is to aid priority setting in health care at the global level by collecting statistics on the degree to which different diseases represent a burden to mankind in terms of the number of people affected, life years lost, and losses in quality of life. Burden of Disease is estimated by assigning disability weights to different kinds of illness. The weights use the same 0–1 value scale as the QALY approach, except that the scale is reversed, so that zero represents "no burden" and unity "maximum burden" (equivalent to "as bad as being dead"). The weights are used in combination with age weights to translate individual life scenarios into a number of Disability Adjusted Life Years (DALYs).

Apart from the age weighting, DALYs are conceptually equivalent to QALYs, inasmuch as they combine reductions in morbidity and mortality in a single value index. Initially, disability weights were established by scoring diseases on a rating scale (World Bank 1993). Later, the developers of DALYs came to the conclusion that rating-scale scores have insufficient meaning for policy-making and that the person trade-off is a more appropriate valuation technique, given that DALYs are supposed to aid resource allocation decisions (Murray 1996). The Burden of Disease Project, in other words, is on the same track as the one I am pursuing in this book. A meeting in Geneva in 1995, at which health workers from various countries used the person trade-off to score a series of diseases in terms of severity, produced health-state valuations with fairly strong upper-end compression, although not quite as strong a those in Table 14 above, see Table 15 (Murray 1996).

It is beyond the scope of this book to examine the DALY approach in full detail. The approach will also be under revision in the next few years. I restrict myself to noting one feature of the approach that should be given further attention (Arnesen and Nord, in press). For a discussion of various other potential problems, the reader is referred to Anand and Hansson (1997).

Person trade-off valuations of health states are done in two different ways in the GBD project. Take, for example, the state "blindness."

Table 15. *Severity weights in Global Burden of Disease Study*

Severity weights	Indicator conditions
0.00–0.02	Vitiligo on face, weight-for-height less than 2 SDs
0.02–0.12	Watery diarrhea, severe sore throat, severe anemia
0.12–0.24	Radius fracture in a stiff cast, infertility, erectile dysfunction, rheumatoid arthritis, angina
0.24–0.36	Below-the-knee amputation, deafness
0.36–0.50	Rectovaginal fistula, mild mental retardation, Down syndrome
0.50–0.70	Unipolar major depression, blindness, paraplegia
0.70–1.00	Active psychosis, dementia, severe migraine, quadriplegia

First, subjects are asked what is referred to as "PTO1" (although in more words): Project A can extend the life of 1,000 healthy people by one year, while project B can extend the life of X blind people by one year. What must X be for you to consider the two projects equally valuable? Then subjects are asked "PTO2": Project A can extend the life of 1,000 healthy people by one year, while project B can give Y people their eyesight back for one year. What must Y be for you to consider the two projects equally valuable?

Assume that the median answer to PTO1 is 2,000. That implies a value for "blindness" of 0.5 ($1000 \times 1.0 = 2000 \times 0.5$). Assume that the median answer to PTO2 is 4,000. That implies a value for "blindness" of 0.75 ($1000 \times 1.0 = 4000 \times [1 - 0.75]$).

Invariably (and unsurprisingly, given our general knowledge about framing effects in preference measurement), PTO1 and PTO2 produce different health-state values. In the GBD project, it is assumed that in calculations of burden of disease or cost-effectiveness, a single value for each health state is required. In a second step of the valuation process, subjects are therefore instructed to adjust their initial responses to PTO1 and PTO2 so that they yield the same values.

The first problem with this is that, in the construction of PTO1, it seems to have been taken for granted that subjects will find it less valuable to extend the life of disabled people than to extend the life of healthy people. This shows up in the starting point of the exercise: 1,000 healthy versus 2,000 blind people. Why doesn't it start with 1,000 versus 1,000? There is no mention of the ethical argument in favor of regarding all lives as equally valuable (at least, all lives above some minimum level of functioning and well-being). Altogether the question seems to *invite* responses that run counter to this basic egalitarian argument.

The second problem is that it is very difficult for subjects doing valuations in the GBD project to stick to the egalitarian argument even if they should happen to think about it and agree with it, since they are forced to reach numerical consistency between PTO1 and PTO2. In practice, we must assume that it means reaching a compromise between the two initial valuations. This compromise is conceptually unclear.

The devaluation, imbedded in the DALY PTO-procedure, of life-extending interventions for disabled people was criticized by Anand and Hanson (1997). Murray and Acharya later defended it explicitly, claiming that they had support across various groups of people who had been invited to discuss the issue (Murray and Acharya 1997, p. 726). The odd thing, though, is that in actual calculations of burden of disease in terms of DALYs, lost-life years in disabled people are in fact counted as heavily as lost-life years in healthy people. The severity weights obtained by PTO1 and PTO2 are used only to quantify the burden of living with different kinds of illness. So the forced consistency between PTO1 and PTO2 is completely unwarranted. I submit that it is a heritage from utilitarian thinking in the QALY approach, in which one single value for each health state seemed natural, and in which the equal valuation of life for disabled people was not recognized as a salient societal concern. Hopefully this weakness in the present DALY valuation procedure will be removed during the revision process that is now taking place.

6.5 TOWARD COST-VALUE ANALYSIS

The values suggested in the Rules of Thumb and in the Norwegian valuation table are based on scattered person trade-off data that are available at present. They are open to debate and modification when further evidence so dictates. Indeed, in the time that passes from when these words were written until they are read, more person trade-off data will most likely have been published in a number of countries, particularly in relation to ongoing work with the estimation of Burden of Disease in terms of DALYs. The point here is not to present final numerical answers, but rather to demonstrate the feasibility of an alternative approach to health outcome valuation, in which the numerical ambitions of health economists are upheld even if their conventional techniques for establishing numerical values for health outcomes are abandoned.

In principle, person trade-off–based health-state values can be used in a multiplicative valuation formula for health-care outcomes, in which the number of years that patients get to enjoy given outcomes are another factor. The valuation model would then be like a QALY model, the only difference being that the quality adjustment would be based on person trade-off judgments rather than on utility assessments.

However, as noted above, the functional relationship between duration of effect and societal value is really not known at present. The assumption in the QALY approach of proportionality, or close to proportionality, between these two factors lacks empirical basis. The substitution of person trade-off–based health-state values for utility-based ones of course does not resolve this part of the total valuation problem. It only provides a more accurate description of how society's valuation of outcomes is affected by the severity of the patients' initial condition and the degree of functional improvement and/or symptom relief. This is an important methodological advance in itself. It could, for instance, be useful in comparisons of outcomes the durations of which exceed a certain threshold value, say ten to twenty years, assuming that society will tend not to worry about differences in duration beyond such a time horizon. In such contexts, where "all else is equal," as economists like to say, person trade-off–based health-state values as shown in Table 14 allow health-care interventions to be compared in terms of input–output ratios that have precisely the properties that cost-effectiveness ratios in general are supposed to have. To see this, consider an intervention A that costs 20,000 dollars per patient and typically takes patients from level 5 to level 3. The value increment is then 0.19 on the 0–1 scale (0.99 − 0.80). The input–output ratio is 20.000/0.19, that is, 105,000 dollars per unit of increment in value. Consider another intervention B that costs 50,000 dollars and typically takes patients from level 8 to level 5. The value increment is 0.80. The input–output ratio is 50,000/0.80, that is, 60,000 dollars per unit of increment in value. So, all else being equal, intervention B has a better input–output ratio, due to a favorable person trade-off on the value side (0.80:0.19 = 4,2) which more than compensates for the unfavorable person trade-off on the cost side (50,000: 20,000 = 2,5).

While this in essence is a kind of cost-effectiveness analysis, I suggest "cost-value analysis" as a name for it (Nord 1993a; Nord et al. 1999), to emphasize the difference between this approach and the QALY approach with respect to the underlying measurement of value. In principle, policymakers could use such cost-value analysis to aid decisions about allocating scarce health-care resources across activity areas. A hypothetical example is given in the Annex ("An Example of Cost-Value Analysis").

I repeat the advantage of this approach: The value numbers derive from a measurement operation that matches precisely what the numbers are supposed to express in cost-effectiveness analysis, namely person trade-offs on the value side. The numbers encapsulate concerns not only for outcome size, that is, the amount of health produced by an intervention, but also for fairness across patients with different severity of condition and different potentials for health. The numbers are comprehensive, in the sense that they cover the whole valuation space from life-saving procedures to small functional improvements. And finally, the numbers can eventually be used in a more comprehensive multiplicative valuation model, which, for instance, includes a parameter covering societal concerns for duration, when data from empirical research makes this justified. Such a model could formally be identical to the conventional QALY model. But its basic measurement concept would be societal value rather than individual utility. To emphasize this, I think it would be a good idea to use the term "cost-value analysis" also for cost-effectiveness analysis based on such a wider valuation model.

Regarding the estimation of other parameters in a wider model, it should be noted that when the purpose of a multifactorial model is to establish person trade-offs on the value side that are comparable to person trade-offs on the production side, the partial relationship between total value and each and every factor in the valuation function needs to be determined by means of societal person trade-off judgments. To see this, consider for instance a model in which value is specified as proportional to duration (the number of years that patients get to enjoy a health improvement). This would imply that, all else being equal, an intervention A the effects of which last twenty years would be valued twice as highly as an intervention B with a ten-year effect. This again would imply a person trade-off between these two interventions of $1A = 2B$. Whether or not this is consistent with societal preferences can only be established by asking representatives of society what they think the person trade-off between these two interventions should be. If the implied person trade-off is not consistent with the directly measured one, then the role of the duration factor in the value function would have to be changed accordingly. This is the same as saying that, ultimately, the functional relationship between duration and value needs to be determined by means of person trade-off questions. The same would be true of such factors as patients' age, distance in time, and uncertainty. There have already been studies in which the person trade-off technique has been used to establish the significance of such additional factors (Olsen 1994; Nord et al. 1996).

At this point readers may feel that I am placing an enormous load on one single measurement technique, namely person trade-off questions, in seeking a way out of the problems associated with the QALY approach to valuing health care. Actually, this is not a choice I am making as a matter of subjective preference. Rather, I am claiming that the person trade-off approach to measurement is necessitated logically by the essence of the problem that cost-effectiveness analysis in health care purports to resolve, which is to compare trade-offs in production with trade-offs in value across different areas of activity. To be comparable, these trade-offs must be expressed in equal terms. Trade-offs in production are expressed in terms of numbers of persons treated. Propositions about trade-offs in value must then be in terms of numbers of persons treated as well. There is no way of knowing whether such propositions are valid other than by, at some stage, directly asking representatives of society person trade-off questions.

Person trade-off measurements may be supported by other approaches. A case in point here is the technique for measuring concerns for equity suggested by Dolan (1998). As noted earlier, he found that subjects tended to regard an improvement in one type of patients (A) from utility level 0.2 to 0.4 as equally valuable as an improvement in an other type of patients (B) from 0.4 to 0.8. According to these subjects, the person trade-off on the value side between these two interventions is thus 1:1. A QALY model would capture this if the utility gain from 0.2 to 0.4 was assigned a severity weight twice as high as that of the utility gain from 0.4 to 0.8, for instance, as follows:

$$QALY(A) = (0.4-0.2) \times 0.8 = 0.16$$
$$QALY(B) = (0.8-0.4) \times 0.4 = 0.16$$

(Implies that the person trade-off according to the QALY calculation is 1:1.)

From this one could proceed to inferring the value of, for instance, an improvement in a third type of patients (C) from 0.4 to 0.6:

$$QALY(C) = (0.6-0.4) \times 0.4 = 0.08$$
Implication: PTO A:C = PTO B:C = 1:2

It would be interesting to see the extent to which data of this kind fit with data from direct person trade-off measurements.

In the following sections I address some of the challenges and problems associated with a person trade-off based approach to cost-value analysis of health care and place the use of such analysis in a larger policy context.

6.6 CONSTRUCTING A COMPREHENSIVE VALUE TABLE

The numbers in Table 14 are supposed to help evaluators assign values to health outcomes for use in cost-value analyses. The idea is that the evaluator should decide at what level of severity a given patient group typically belongs at the outset and to which level these patients would be taken by the intervention that is to be evaluated. Then the value of the improvement can be read out of the table. However, as it stands, the table has quite limited direct applicability inasmuch as it refers only to a very limited set of levels of severity, and also to a very limited set of conditions of disability that mainly have to do with mobility. They say nothing about what values should be assigned to conditions that involve other kinds of health problems. In other words, to make cost-value analysis practically useful across the whole range of health services requires a much more comprehensive instrument for assigning person trade-off values.

Such an instrument would need a descriptive system of the kind occurring in multi-attribute utility instruments used in the QALY field. A number of these are listed in Table 4 (Chapter 4). The EuroQol instrument is an example. It has five dimensions for health (mobility, self-care, usual activity, pain/discomfort, and mood) and three levels of functioning on each of these dimensions (no problems, some problems, extreme problems/unable to). Any diagnostic group can be described in terms of these dimensions and levels. The EuroQol Instrument provides a utility (based on the rating scale or the time trade-off) for all 243 theoretically possible combinations of dimensions and levels within this descriptive system. A number of these theoretical combinations are unrealistic, like, for instance, "being unable to move about" and at the same time "not having any problems with usual activities." Also, as argued earlier, the meaningfulness and validity of the utility numbers are questionable. If, however, all feasible combinations were assigned a value based on person trade-off measurements, evaluators would have at hand an instrument that would make sensible cost-value analysis doable for a very large number of health-care interventions.

Whichever descriptive system is chosen (and there may be a need for an even more detailed one than that of the EuroQol), the assignment of values requires data collection in two steps (Nord et al. 1999). The first is to determine the loss of quality of life associated with different states in the descriptive system. As argued in Chapter 5, these data should be elicited from patients who actually are in those states rather than by asking samples of the general population to imagine themselves in different states of illness. The second step is to discover the person trade-offs that society wishes to make between interventions for patients in the different states of the descriptive system, given the data that have been collected on quality of life. These *distributive judgments* need to be elicited from the potential users of the health-care system – that is, from representative samples of the general population – after these have been given the quality-of-life information. In other words, the person trade-off preferences should be elicited from informed members of the public, and the information they are given should derive from patients' own direct experience.

6.7 MEASUREMENT PROBLEMS

The quality-of-life data required for this two-step approach may be of various kinds. It is important to note, however, that they need not be in terms of utilities. The requirement in cost-value analysis that values be expressed at a cardinal level is accommodated by the person trade-off questions in step two of the procedure. For practical purposes, ordinal quality of life data are surely sufficient to give members of the general public a clear picture of how bad different states of illness are felt relative to each other. A large body of such ordinal data already exists (see the literature on quality of life in patients reviewed in Chapter 5). Nonetheless, the amount of additional empirical work needed to cover the whole descriptive area of a multidimensional system like, for instance, the EuroQol should not be underestimated.

Like any other technique for eliciting preferences from people, the person trade-off has to be reliable and valid. Since few researchers have used the technique up to now, there is very limited evidence of its psychometric properties. However, some problems have been identified.

In one small-scale study (reported in Nord 1995), individual responses to person trade-off questions were found to have low test–retest reliability, due to the fact that subjects are not used to thinking of values in health care in precise numerical terms. When "forced" to express value judgments in person trade-off terms, they therefore respond somewhat arbitrarily. Fortunately the measurement error introduced by this arbitrariness becomes less of a problem when the focus is on average judgments in large groups of subjects, since positive and negative random errors then tend to cancel each other out.

Responses to questions about preferences for resource allocation are sensitive to how they are asked. Examples of this have been given earlier. For instance, Ubel (1997) found that small changes in the phrasing of response options that I had originally formulated strongly affected the degree to which subjects' emphasized severity of illness relative to capacity to benefit from treatment. Similarly, Pinto and Perpinan (in press) found that the emphasis that subjects placed on post-treatment state when valuing life-extending procedures depended on whether or not post-treatment state was focused upon explicitly as an independent concern.

A study of the person trade-off technique showed that questions that explicitly indicated different ethical positions that the subjects might want to adopt produced different responses than questions that simply described competing programs and left it entirely to the subjects to find out how they might want to think about prioritization problems. In another study, responses proved to be extremely sensitive to the starting points used in the stepwise numerical measurement procedure. For instance, if A and B were two outcomes, subjects were initially asked which they preferred of ten As and ten Bs. If they said ten As, they were asked to choose between ten As and a hundred Bs, and then gradually their point of indifference would be circled in. It was later discovered that in a case where A was considered more valuable than B, if one started with ten As versus a hundred Bs (instead of ten versus ten), the subjects tended to end up at a much higher indifference value. (Both these studies are reported in Nord 1995.)

Person trade-off questions evoke ethical considerations, which probably vary more across social subgroups than do perceptions of the disutility of illness. Responses to person trade-off questions may therefore be sensitive to *whom* one asks. Person trade-off studies have generally involved too small numbers of subjects to allow for subgroup comparisons. However, the previously cited study of preferences for resource allocation in a sample of Norwegian politicians (Nord 1993b) indirectly sheds some light on the issue. The subjects were asked to choose between a utilitarian and an egalitarian response in five different contexts in which a given amount of resources could be divided between two different groups of patients A and B. The first context (I) was "equally ill patients, where more could be done for A than for B." The second context (II) was "group B more ill than A, but more could be done for A than for B." The third, fourth, and fifth contexts (III–V) were "20- versus 60-year olds", "60- versus 70-year olds" and "70- versus 80-year olds." In each of these contexts, to give priority to the first group in the pair would be a utilitarian preference. Table 16 shows the percentage of utilitarian responses among conservatives and social democrats, respectively. The inclination toward utilitarianism was systematically much stronger in conservatives. It is reasonable to assume that this difference would also show up in person trade-off questions.

Ubel et al. (1996) found that responses to person trade-off questions do not follow rules of transitivity. For instance, if one A was judged as valuable as ten Bs and one B was judged as valuable as twenty Cs, then theoretically one A ought to be judged as valuable as two hundred Cs. In effect, the directly measured person trade-off between "distant outcomes" – in this case A and C – tended to be much lower than what was indicated by multiplying trade-offs between a sequence of "neighboring outcomes" (in this case, A/B and B/C). Pinto (1997) made similar observations.

Table 16. *Percentage of utilitarian preferences in five different choice contexts*

Context:	I	II	III	IV	V
Conservatives	52	21	50	20	27
Social democrats	18	11	28	8	15

These various findings indicate that, while the person trade-off approach to valuing health outcomes has great theoretical validity, it would be naive to think that it is an easy way to obtain accurate numerical representations of societal preferences for resource allocation. The approach is associated with a number of sources of measurement error that need to be carefully addressed by researchers in the field. Some sensible measurement strategies are already indicated at this point: The technique needs to be applied in fairly large groups of subjects to keep random measurement error at an acceptable level and to avoid political biases. To control for framing effects, it seems important to take subjects through a multistep procedure, in which they are induced to consider carefully the various arguments that might be relevant in each comparison and to reconsider initial responses in the light of their implications. In other words, the investigator ideally should be seeking to establish a "reflective equilibrium" (Rawls 1971) in his or her subjects. Start point bias may possibly be kept at a minimum by presenting the subjects first with a very low equivalence number and then with a very high one, and then by "ping-ponging" between narrowing extremes until a point of indifference is found. It is of course very difficult to fulfill all these requirements using self-administered questionnaires; direct, personal communication seems necessary. The individual interviews reported by Rosser and Kind (1978) are one example of how this may be done. Seminars described in Nord (1994b) and Murray and Lopez (1996) are other examples.

While the framing details of person trade-off questions should remain open to debate and experimenting, the methodological problems mentioned above can hardly be regarded as potentially fatal to the relevance of the person trade-off approach itself. That would be like losing something in a dark part of the street and then looking for it underneath the nearest lamp post simply because there is more light there. Given the fact that comparison of person trade-offs is the essence of cost-effectiveness analysis, there is no way that asking person trade-off questions can be avoided. Measurement problems should therefore not be regarded as potentially fatal, but rather as problems that researchers should address and learn to master as well as possible.

6.8 THE RELEVANCE OF COST-VALUE ANALYSIS IN PRACTICAL DECISION MAKING

The optimistic message of this book is that, even if it requires extensive and cumbersome data collection, it is possible to model population preferences for resource allocation in health care in terms of meaningful and evidence-based person trade-off numbers. The numbers allow different health-care procedures to be compared in terms of their cost-value ratios. However, some words must be said about the potential use of such ratios. In what way can they be helpful in practice? There are three aspects of this problem that I wish to address here. One has to do with the usefulness of numbers as opposed to verbal information, another with the different levels at which resource allocation decisions are made, and a third with the opportunities for sharing resources among different potential recipients rather than "letting the winners take all." Let us look at each of these in turn.

6.8.1 *The Usefulness of Numbers*

The numbers in Table 14 are supposed to express the trade-off between severity of initial state and treatment effect in prioritizing between different patient groups. The table begs a question. Determining the trade-off between severity and treatment effect is essentially a question of ethical judgment. Normally we leave this kind of question open to continuous political debate and expect politicians to make decisions in specific cases based on reponsible, overall judgment. In the light of this, does society at all need a table like Table 14?

I believe the answer to this is yes. To see why, we must bear in mind that, even in ethical matters, politicians need guidelines that reflect the views of the community at large, facilitate consistency in decision making over time, and protect against ad hoc influences of media, patient organizations, lobbyists, and others. In the health-care sector, the latter point is not the least important. The question is therefore really whether there is any advantage in expressing ethical guidelines in *numerical* terms.

A necessary condition for this to be the case is that the numbers are *meaningful* to potential users. In the context of health status indices and quality-adjusted life years this may be problematic, as quality of life is not directly observable and very few people – if any – use numerical scales in everyday situations when thinking of or expressing quality of life. However, meaning is not a problem in Table 14. The numbers are expressions of relative value, based directly on responses to meaningful equivalence of numbers questions.

Given this meaningfulness of the numbers, the argument in favor of them is that guidelines are more helpful the more *precisely* they describe the intentions of those who gave them. A guideline saying, for instance, that "operations costing more than US $300,000 should normally not be undertaken" is more helpful than a guideline saying that "very expensive operations should normally not be undertaken." Inclusion of the term "normally" makes both statements guidelines that leave room for decision makers' discretion. But the numerical formulation gives a much more precise impression of the intentions of the guiding body than does the verbal one. Similarly, a guideline saying that "outcome X is normally appreciated ten times as much by society as outcome Y" is a more precise representation of social preferences than a guideline saying that "outcome X is normally much more appreciated than outcome Y." Moving to this higher level of precision in the communication of *intentions in guidelines* does not change the status of the guidelines as such. Users of the guidelines may still – and should be encouraged to – make necessary adjustments in actual decisions.

6.8.2 Decision Levels

As noted in Chapter 2, decisions about resource allocation are made at a number of different levels in a health-care system, including the budget level, the admission level, and the clinical level. I argued that economic analysis primarily has a role to play at the budget level.

A natural question to ask is what health economists in general have to say about this. Do they recommend that economic decision rules be applied equally rigorously at all these levels? If not, for which level or levels are economic evaluation models primarily recommended?

There is in fact very little theoretical discussion of this issue in the health economics literature. What we mainly find are statements that suggest what has been in the back of the minds of various writers in the field.

Generally speaking, the cost-per-QALY decision-making rule is strongly associated with *program evaluation*. This is evaluation at the group budget level and is essentially what QALY league tables are all about. It is the only level referred to, for instance, by Torrance (1986),

Drummond et al. (1987), and Jönsson (1990). Jönsson explicitly states that "economic evaluations are mainly undertaken at the program level. . . . It is . . . hardly ethical to conduct explicit studies of individual patients" (p. 93).

But not all health economists are as conservative as Jönsson. According to Weinstein and Stason (1977), "the basic analytic framework should be useful to a variety of decision makers, including physicians, hospitals and insurance programs" (p. 721). Weinstein (1981) claims that "the findings of cost-effectiveness analysis may be useful in decision making not only for populations of patients, but also for individual patients" (p. 310). Williams (1987a) speaks about determining "treatment capacity" and "which technology to provide and which not to provide," which is much the same as group-level budgeting and program evaluation, but he also asks, "Who is to live?" and answers, "Those for whom we can do the most good per unit of resources used" (p. 34). This formulation certainly does not exclude the admission level. Even less so does the claim that the cost per QALY approach can be "useful for selecting patients within a diagnostic group" (p. 35) and the recommendation that "clinicians select the particular patients who will benefit most from the technologies that are affordable" (p. 36). In a later article Williams also defends the view that "it is the doctor's duty to take cost into account when deciding what course of action to recommend for the patients" (1988c, p. 1183). This is in fact the clinical level. Similarly, Torrance (1987) includes "clinical decision analysis" when indicating the potential applications of the utility approach.

Altogether, I do not think health economists have been particularly careful in pointing out the limitations of economic evaluation in terms of areas of application. On the contrary, they have tended to leave their readers with the impression that economic evaluation has an important role to play at all the three levels of decision making listed above. In my opinion, this is an unrealistic ambition, which probably has contributed to the rise of skepticism toward the use of economic evaluation models even in decision contexts where the models really could be helpful (Smith 1987).

Personally, I was led to think in some detail about these issues when I was invited to a workshop in Santiago de Chile in October 1994. A sharp conflict had arisen a few months before between the minister of health in Chile and the Chilean Medical Association. The minister complained in public that the productivity of doctors' hours

Figure 3. *Differences in values between health professionals and health economists*

	"Presence"	Severity	Treatability	Cost
Health professionals	+ + +	+ + +	+ +	+
Health economists	+	+	+ + +	+ + +

in the Chilean Public Health Service had dropped in the years 1989–1993 in terms of numbers of surgical procedures performed and patients treated. The Medical Association offered a number of explanations of why this had happened. In particular they claimed that in the late 1980s a need had accumulated to increase the quality and safety of services after several preceding years during which funding had been cut and the use of doctors' time in many procedures had been reduced to unacceptably low levels.

In an effort to reconcile the conflicting parties, the Panamerican Health Organization organized a workshop, to which representatives of central and local health authorities were invited along with representatives of various health professions, to discuss how productivity in health care can be measured, monitored, and enhanced.

One of the problems addressed at the workshop was the tendency for health professionals and health economists to emphasize different factors in matters of prioritizing in health care. While the former are highly concerned with how severely ill the patients are and with the obligation they have toward the patients immediately before them, economists are more concerned with how much can be done for the patients, what this will cost, and hence how many people one can manage to help with a given budget. Figure 3 illustrates this difference in values.

A challenge in resource allocation in health care then seems to be to find a way of increasing the role of economic evaluation without setting aside long-standing ethics in the health professions.

It seems to me that the key to achieving this lies precisely in recognizing the existence of different decision levels in resource allocation. Health professionals are primarily involved in decision making at the admission and clinical levels. I believe much conflict could be avoided

Figure 4. *Illustration of distribution of treatment capacity when cost-value considerations are disregarded*

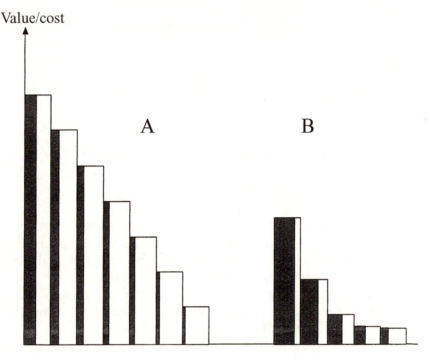

if a process aiming at increasing the role of economic evaluation were to focus primarily on decisions at the group budget level.

Figures 4 and 5 illustrate the implications of such a strategy. Assume two different services, A and B. Assume also that there exists some accepted way of measuring value in health care, for instance, in terms of person trade-off–based values as suggested above. The patients seeking each of the services A and B vary with respect to both costs and value of treatment. In Figure 4, the patients seeking each service are grouped according to their value-cost ratio. Each column represents 1,000 patients. Total demand per year is 12,000 patients (seven coloumns in A and five columns in B). There is capacity to treat only 5,000. Figure 4 illustrates an initial situation, in which the distribution of this capacity has been decided on other grounds than that of cost-value analysis. The shaded area in each column shows the share of patients in that group who receive treatment. In the chosen example, coverage is better in service B than in service A, even though the overall value-cost ratio is higher in service

A than B. Also, while coverage within each service tends to be higher the higher the value-cost ratio, patients are admitted from all sub-groups (since cost-value analysis is not strictly applied).

Figure 5 shows the consequences of dividing resources between the two services (the budget level) according to the principles of cost-value analysis, while leaving the distribution of resources within each service (the admission level) unchanged. If total treatment capacity is still to be 5,000 patients, decision makers at the budget level will want to give priority to the first four groups (columns) in service A and the first group (column) in service B (each column represents 1000 patients). They will divide the total budget accordingly between A and B. Figure 5 illustrates the result of this reallocation at the group budget level, assuming that admission practices within each service do not change. There is now better coverage in service A than in service B (see the shaded areas), and the total value produced is clearly greater than in Figure 4 (because of the generally more favorable value-cost ratios in service A).

Figure 5. *Distribution of treatment capacity when cost-value considerations are taken into account*

Value/cost

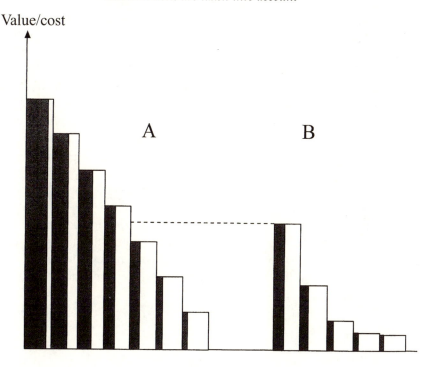

The example illustrates that, without imposing economic thinking on health professionals at the admission level or the bedside level, it is conceivable that considerable gains may be achieved by following principles of economic evaluation at the budget level. At least for starters, therefore, it seems like a good idea for health economists to focus more consistently and exclusively on the budget level when advocating and conducting economic evaluation of health care.

Having said this, there is no denying that to refrain from applying evaluation to the admission level and the bedside level obviously means leaving some potential productivity gains unharvested. The rationale for this would be to avoid conflict with medical ethics. But would society at large be happy with this? If not, how could economic evaluation to some extent be introduced, for instance, at the admission level without troubling clinicians unduly?

It seems to me that this very much depends on what kind of principles the *users* of the health services, namely current and potential future patients, would like to see applied. Should the general public want admission decisions to be guided by economic evaluation, then I hypothesize that there is not much of a problem with medical ethics. I believe the ethics of the health professions are formed largely by patients' values and expectations. I do not think it would be very difficult for doctors to set out guidelines for selecting patients that placed greater emphasis, for instance, on costs and treatability *if that was what the public wanted*. If such guidelines were established, and if it were known that they enjoyed public support, then it would also be much easier than it is today for doctors to justify refusals to treat on the grounds of economic evaluation. But again, the important question is whether this *is* what the public wants. On the basis of evidence of the kind presented in Chapter 4, I suspect it is not. This brings me back to my first point: There may be much value to be gained from applying numerical societal value measures to health-care outcomes and from applying cost-value analysis to decision making at the budget level. Such steps toward monitoring and increasing health care productivity ought not to be too hard for doctors to accept. On the other hand, at the end of the day health economists and health authorities may have to accept the fact that economic evaluation should continue to play a limited role in doctors' prioritizing among individual patients.

6.8.3 *Winners Take All?*

I have argued above that cost-value analysis has a role to play primarily in decisions about resource allocation across diagnostic groups. But even in that context there is an important limitation to the relevance of economic evaluation.

Some readers may have noted an inconsistency between the theoretical rationale of the person trade-off approach, on the one hand, and, on the other hand, evidence reported in Chapter 4 on the emphasis that society at large wishes to place on costs – and thereby on the number of people treated – in valuing health programs. Let us say that treatment A costs five times as much as treatment B. So for each person given treatment A one can alternatively give five other people treatment B. Assume that a person trade-off measurement shows that one person receiving A is considered equivalent to three people receiving B. The person trade-off data then suggest that resources should be allocated to treatment B rather than to treatment A. Patients in need of treatment A would then effectively be losing in the competition for scarce resources *because of their high cost*. While this of course is unsurprising and probably also unproblematic to most economists, it is in fact precisely this implication of cost-effectiveness analysis that is countered by the evidence reported in Chapter 4. According to that evidence, most people seem prepared to make quite significant sacrifices in terms of the total number of people treated by the health-care system in order to allow the system to treat fairly those who happen to have a high-cost illness.

Does that mean that the person trade-off approach itself is based on a false assumption, namely that the societal value of a program is proportional to the number of people who get to enjoy a particular benefit? In other words, is person trade-off based cost-value analysis also misconceived? Or is some sense in the person trade-off approach reconcilable with the view that society seems to hold on the role of costs in prioritizing?

I think the answer to the latter question is yes. The problem is not that person trade-off questions pick up false values. Rather, there has been a lack of recognition among economists as to what kind of decisions cost-effectiveness analysis are primarily relevant for.

The logic of cost-effectiveness analysis is really this. If two programs are competing for a given amount of resources, *and one cannot divide these resources between the two programs but has to pick one and only one of them*, then one should choose the program that has the better cost-effectiveness ratio. Such indivisibility of resources across programs may certainly occur in real-world decision contexts, for instance because programs have high set-up costs in terms of buildings, medical equipment, and training of personnel, and relatively low marginal costs of treating additional patients. *In such "either-or" contexts, cost-value analysis based on person trade-off values may provide a valid picture of societal preferences.*

However, far from all resource allocation problems demand "either-or" solutions. For instance, the question may be to which diagnostic groups a given medical facility with a given staff should devote its time, assuming fairly constant marginal costs per patient treated within each group. In such a context the concerns for fairness reported in Chapter 4 apply. People do not then want the facility to concentrate 100 percent on those groups who have the better ratios between costs and value and to refuse treatment completely to groups who happen to score less well in this respect. They would rather see some sharing of resources, for instance as indicated in Table 12 in Chapter 4, as a compromise between economic ex ante rationality on the one hand and concerns for people's ex post emotional reactions to complete denial of treatment on the other. Cost-value ratios may provide some help to decision makers in judging how society would like to see the resources shared among groups. But it is important to acknowledge that the role of cost-value ratios in this decision-making context probably will be quite modest.

There is an interesting parallel here to a reaction that I have often encountered among health-care personnel when I have lectured about cost-effectiveness analysis. "These rankings of diagnostic groups that follow from your analysis," they have told me, "have no place in our everyday practice. We don't think in terms of either-or. We try to do something for everybody. That is our obligation." It strikes me that health economists (and here I definitely include myself) have been too slow in appreciating this very basic ethical position. The evidence reported in Chapter 4 suggests that, on this issue, the values of health-care personnel may be quite consistent with the values of the population at large.

6.9 CONCLUSION

Cost-effectiveness analysis has for many years been using a generic measure of value – the QALY – that disregards very significant societal concerns for fairness in health care. Furthermore, it uses the concept of cardinal individual utility, which is not only difficult to measure in an understandable and verifiable way, but also unnecessary to measure when the ultimate goal is to estimate *society's* valuation of health care outcomes. In theory, it is perfectly possible to model society's valuations – in which concerns for both efficiency and fairness are relevant – numerically, and thus to perform a comprehensive kind of cost-effectiveness analysis of health interventions that might suitably be called cost-value analysis. We already have a host of international studies of preferences for resource allocation that allow us roughly to specify such a model. It differs from most existing models for QALY calculations in that it compresses mild and moderate states of illness to the upper end of the 0–1 value scale, so that severity of illness receives much greater weight, and discrimination against patient groups with lesser potentials for health is significantly reduced. The model also restricts the use of health-state values so as to allow for the equal evaluation of life-extending programs for healthy and disabled people.

Much work remains to be done to refine this model. As the work progresses, decision makers hopefully will find the model more and more useful as an aid to reflection about setting priorities across a wide range of health interventions that compete for scarce resources in public and private health insurance plans. But I emphasize that this is for time to show. As indicated in the preceding sections, a number of psychological and organizational factors in practice limit the actual use of results from formal, quantitative cost-effectiveness analysis in health-care decision making. Some of these factors must be respected.

Annex: An Example of Cost-Value Analysis

Assume that a psychiatric outpatient clinic applies for funds to establish a treatment program for people with chronic anxiety. The treatment will consist of counseling twice a week for three years. A typical patient in the target group is a woman between the ages of thirty and forty who is on disability leave from work. Her anxiety is "bearable" at home, but the patient needs to be accompanied whenever she leaves the house. Assume that it is documented that the therapy will make it possible for the patient to get around alone, function in most social situations, and be partially fit to resume employment, although she will still have symptoms. The treatment will cost approximately US$10,000 per patient.

In order to judge the degree to which the program deserves funding the responsible public health authority compares its estimated results with results in three other areas of health care where there also is a demand for more resources. One is a not yet implemented preventive screening program, and the two others are areas of surgery where there are considerable waiting lists.

The screening program has been proposed for a congenital trait that leads to total invalidization around the age of thirty to forty unless prophylactic treatment is undertaken in time. Assume that the trait occurs in one out of every thousand individuals. Testing for the trait costs US $20,00 per person. Assuming (for simplicity) 100 percent sensitivity and specificity of the test, each positive finding then costs US $20,000. Assume furthermore a 100 percent effective treatment that costs US $10,000. The cost of preventing one case of total invalidization is then 10,000 + 20,000 = US $30,000.

The second area of comparison is a common orthopedic procedure, namely an operation for hallux valgus (crooked big toe). A typical patient is a woman between the ages of sixty and seventy. She has slight-to-moderate pain, which increases with movement, and has difficulties when climbing stairs or going outside. The operation costs US $1,000 and generally yields complete cure.

The third area of comparison is bypass operations for people with moderate angina. The typical patient is a man between sixty-five and seventy years old. He has chronic chest pain, which curtails his movement outdoors, restricts strenuous activities at home, and wakes him at night. Side-effects from his medication are headache, nausea, and fatigue. The operation costs US $15,000 and usually results in freedom from symptoms and return to normal function except in cases of extreme exertion.

In the cost-value analysis of the four programs, the before-and-after situation for each type of patient is placed on the severity-scale shown earlier in Table 13. The placements will be based on data on the health-related quality of life in each of the patient groups in question (with and without intervention) compared with data on health-related quality of life in people with functional problems as those indicated at the different levels in table 13. The placements on the scale, society's valuation of the improvements of function from the different treatments (from Table 14), the costs of treatment, and the relationship between costs and values are shown in Table 17. The analysis suggests that the cost-value ratio is at least as favorable for the suggested treatment for patients with chronic anxiety as for the operation for patients with moderate angina, but not as favorable as the screening program and the operation for hallux valgus. The comparison gives a rough estimate of the priority rating that these four programs should have relative to each other when competing for resources to increase treatment capacity. The rating takes into account treatment costs and

Table 17. *Cost-value analysis of four programs*

Program	Severity Before	After	Value	Cost	Cost-value ratio (value per US $ 1 million)
Anxiety	4	2–3	0.07–0.08	10,000	7–8
Screening	7	1	0.60	30,000	20
Angina	4	1–2	0.08	15,000	5–6
Hallux valgus	3	1	0.01	1,000	10

systematically collected data on public preferences for priority setting. The values reflect, not only concerns for utility gains, but also concerns for the severity of the patients' pretreatment condition. They disregard differences in age and duration of effect, on the assumption that people do not care about differences in duration when duration is as long as it is in all these four programs. Because of the way in which severity and duration are handled in the analysis, the values purport to be more appropriate than values in terms of QALYs. The estimates may stimulate thought and thus be a useful piece of information for health authorities when they consider the application for funding of the program for patients with anxiety.

References

Anand, S., and Hanson, K. 1997. Disability-adjusted life years: a critical review. *Journal of Health Economics* 16:685–702.

Arnesen, T. M., and Nord, E. The value of DALY life. *British Medical Journal* 1999 (in press).

Björk, S., and Rosen, P. 1993. Prioriteringar i sjukvården. (Prioritizing in health care.) *IHE arbetsrapport* 1 (1993). Lund: Institutet for helso- och sjukvårdsekonomi.

Bombardier, C., et al. 1982. Comparison of three preference measurement methodologies in the evaluation of a functional status index. In R. B. Deber and G. G. Thompson, eds., *Choice in Health Care*. University of Toronto, Department of Health Administration.

Bråkenhielm, C. R. 1990. Vård på lika vilkår (Health care on equal terms). In J. Caltorp and C. R. Bråkenhielm, eds., *Vårdens pris* (The price of care). Stockholm: Verbum forlag.

Brock, D. 1988. Ethical issues in recipient selection for organ transplantation. In D. Mathieu, *Organ substitution technology: Ethical, legal and public policy issues.* Boulder: Westview Press.

Brock, D. 1995. Justice and the ADA: Does prioritizing and rationing health care discriminate against the disabled? *Social Philosophy and Policy* 12:159–184.

Broome, J. 1988. Goodness, fairness and QALYs. In J. M. Bell and S. Mendus, eds., *Philosophy and medical welfare*. Cambridge University Press.

Busschbach, J. J. V.; Hessing, D. J.; and de Charro, F. T. 1993. The utility of health at different stages in life: A quantitative approach. *Social Science & Medicine* 37:153–158.

Buxton, M.; Ashby, J.; and O'Hanlon, M. 1987. Alternative methods of valuing health states. Mimeograph. Brunel University, Health Economics Research Group.

Callahan, D. 1994. Setting mental health priorities: Problems and possibilities. *The Milbank Quarterly* 72:451–470.

Calman, K. C. 1984. Quality of life in cancer patients – an hypothesis. *Journal of Medical Ethics* 10:124–127.

Campbell, A., and Gillett, G. 1993. Justice and the right to health care. In

Ethical issues in defining core services. Wellington: The National Advisory Committee on Core Health and Disability Support Services.

Cassileth, B. R., et al. 1984. Psychosocial status in chronic illness. A comparative analysis of six diagnostic groups. *New England Journal of Medicine* 311: 506–511.

Charny, M. C.; Lewis, P. A.; and Farrow, S. C. 1989. Choosing who shall not be treated in the NHS. *Social Science & Medicine* 28:1331–1338.

Chiang, C. L. 1965. An index of health: Mathematical models. PHS publ. no 1000, ser. 2, no. 5. Washington, DC: US Government Printing Office.

Churchill, D. N.; Morgan, J.; and Torrance, G. W. 1984. Quality of life in end stage renal disease. *Peritoneal Dialysis Bulletin* (Jan–March), 20–23.

Clipp, E. C., and Elder, G. H. 1987. Elderly confidants in geriatric assessment. *Compr Gerontol B* 1, 35–40.

Core Services Committee. 1994. Core Services for 1995/1996. Wellington: Ministry of Health, August.

Cropper, M. L.; Ayede, S. K; and Portney, P. R. 1994. Preferences for life saving programs: How the public discounts time and age. *Journal of Risk and Uncertainty*, 243–265.

Culyer, A. J. 1989. The normative economics of health care finance and provision. *Oxford Review of Economic Policy* 5:34–58.

Culyer, A. J. 1991. Conflicts between equity concepts and efficiency in health: A diagrammatic approach. *Osaka Economic Papers* 40:141–154.

Culyer, A. J.; Lavers, R. J.; and Williams, A. 1971. Social indicators: Health. *Social Trends* 2:31–42.

Daniels, N. 1985. *Just Health Care*. Cambridge, MA: Harvard University Press.

Daniels, N. 1993. Rationing fairly: Programmatic considerations. *Bioethics* 7: 224–233.

Derogatis, L. R.; Abeloff, M. D.; McBeth, C. D. 1976. Cancer patients and their physicians in the perception of psychological symptoms. Psychosomatics 17:197–201.

Dolan, P. 1998. The measurement of individual utility and social welfare. *Health Economics* 17:39–52.

Dolan, P., and Cookson, R. 1998. "Measuring preferences over the distribution of health benefits." Mimeo. University of York, Centre for Health Economics.

Drummond, M. F.; Stoddart, G. L.; and Torrance, G. W. 1987. *Methods for the economic evaluation of health care programmes*. Oxford: Oxford University Press.

Dutch Committee on Choices in Health Care. 1992. *Choices in health care*. Rijswijk: Ministry of Welfare, Health and Cultural Affairs.

Eddy, D. M. 1991. Oregon's Methods: Did cost-effectiveness analysis fail? *Journal of the American Medical Association* 266:2135–2141.

Epstein, A. M., et al. 1989. Using proxies to evaluate quality of life. *Medical Care* 27:S91–S98.

The EuroQol Group. 1990. EuroQol – a new facility for the measurement of health related quality of life. *Health Policy* 16:199–208.

Feeny, D.; Furlong, W.; Boyle, M.; and Torrance, G. W. 1995. Multi-attribute health status classification systems. *Pharmacoeconomics* 7:490–502.

Fowler, F. J.; Cleary, P. D.; Massagli, M. P.; Weissman, J.; and Epstein, A. 1995. The role of reluctance to give up life in the measurement of the value of health states. *Medical Decision Making* 15:195–200.

Froberg, D. G., and Kane, R. L. 1989. Methodology for measuring health-state preferences. *Journal of Clinical Epidemiology* 42:345–354, 459–471, 585–592, 675–685.

Fryback, D. G.; Dasbach, E. J.; Klein, R.; et al. 1993. The Beaver Dam Health Outcomes Study. *Medical Decision Making* 13:89–102.

Garber, A. M.; Weinstein, M. C.; Torrance, G. W.; and Kamlet, M. S. 1996. Theoretical foundations of cost-effectiveness analysis. In Gold et al. 1996 (*see below*).

Gerard, K. 1992. Cost-utility in practice: A policy makers' guide to the state of the art. *Health Policy* 21:249–279.

Gold, M. R.; Siegel, J. E.; Russell, L. B.; and Weinstein, M. C. 1996. *Cost-effectiveness in health and medicine.* New York: Oxford University Press.

Hadorn, D. 1991. Setting health care priorities in Oregon. *JAMA* 265:2218–2225.

Hadorn, D. 1995. Large scale health outcome evaluation: How should quality of life be measured? *Journal of Clinical Epidemiology* 48:607–618.

Harris, J. 1987. QALYfying the value of life. *Journal of Medical Ethics* 13:117–123.

Harsyani, J. C. 1953. Cardinal utility in welfare economics and in the theory of risk taking. *Journal of Political Economy* 61:434–435.

Hawthorne, G., and Richardson, J. 1996. An Australian multi-attribute utility: Rationale and preliminary results. Working paper 49. Melbourne: Centre for Health Program Evaluation.

Johannesson, M., and Johansson, P.-O. 1996. The economics of ageing: On the attitude of Swedish people to the distribution of health care resources between the young and the old. *Health Policy* 37:153–161.

Johannesson, M., and Jönsson, B. 1991. Economic evaluation in health care: Is there a role for cost-benefit analysis? *Health Policy* 17:1–23.

Jonsen, A. 1986. Bentham in a box: Technology assessment and health care allocation. *Law in Medicine and Health Care* 14:172–174.

Jönsson, B. 1990. Quality of life – economic aspects. *Scandinavian Journal of Primary Health Care*, Supplement 1, 93–96.

Kahneman, D., and Tversky, A. 1983. Choices, values and frames. *American Psychology* 39:341–350.

Kamm, F. 1989. The report of the US Task Force on Organ Transplantation: criticisms and alternatives. *Mount Sinae Journal of Medicine* 56:207–220.

Kaplan, R. M. 1989. Health outcome models for policy analysis. *Health Psychology* 8:723–735.

Kaplan, R. M., and Anderson, J. P. 1988. A general health model: Update and applications. *Health Services Research* 23:203–235.

Kind, P.; Rosser, R.; and Williams, A. 1982. Valuations of life: Some psychometric evidence. In M. W. Jones-Lee, ed., *Value of life and safety*. Amsterdam: North Holland Publishing Company.

Knussen, C., and Cunningham, C. C. 1988. Stress, disability and handicap. In S. Fisher and J. Reason, eds., *Handbook of life stress*. New York: Wiley and Sons Ltd.

Llewellyn-Thomas, H. A.; Sutherland, H. J.; and Thiel, E. 1993. Do patients' evaluations of a future health state change when they actually enter that state? *Medical Care* 31:1002–1012.

Lockwood, M. 1988. Quality of life and resource allocation. In J. M. Bell and S. Mendus, eds., *Philosophy and medical welfare*. Cambridge University Press.

Loomes, G., and McKenzie, L. 1989. The use of QALYs in health care decision making. *Social Science & Medicine* 28:299–308.

Magaziner, J.; Simonsick, E. M.; Kashner, T. M.; and Hebel, J. R. 1988. Patient-proxy response comparability on measures of patient health and functional status. *Journal of Clinical Epidemiology* 41:1065–1074.

McCusker, J., and Stoddard, A. M. 1984. Use of a surrogate for the Sickness Impact Profile. *Medical Care* 22:789–795.

Menzel, P. 1990. *Strong medicine*. New York: Oxford University Press.

Menzel, P. 1998. Towards a broader view of values in cost-effectiveness analysis of health care. Hastings Center Report 1999 (in press).

Mooney, G., and Olsen, J. A. 1991. QALYs: Where next? In A. McGuire et al., eds., *Providing health care: The economics of alternative systems of finance and delivery*. Oxford University Press.

Morris, J., and Durand, A. 1989. Category rating methods: Numerical and verbal scales. Mimeo. University of York: Centre for Health Economics.

Mulkay, M.; Ashmore, M.; and Pinch, T. 1987. Measuring the quality of life. *Sociology* 21:541–564.

Mulley, A. G. 1989. Assessing patients' utilities. Can the ends justify the means? *Medical Care* 27:S269–S281.

Murray, C. 1996. Rethinking DALYs. In C. Murray and A. Lopez. *The Global Burden of Disease*. WHO/Harvard University Press.

Murray, C., and Acharya, A. K. 1997. Understanding DALYs. *Journal of Health Economics* 16:703–730.

Murray, C., and Lopez, A. 1996. *The Global Burden of Disease*. WHO/Harvard University Press.

Nord, E. 1989. The significance of contextual factors in valuing health states. *Health policy* 13:189–198.

Nord, E. 1991. The validity of a visual analogue scale in determining social utility weights for health states. *International Journal of Health Planning and Management* 6:234–242.

Nord, E. 1992a. Methods for quality adjustment of life years. *Social Science & Medicine* 34:559–569.

Nord, E. 1992b. Bedømming av pasienters livskvalitet. (Assessing patients' quality of life. A literature review.) Forskningsrapport nr. F1–1992. Oslo: Statens institutt for folkehelse, seksjon for helsetjenesteforskning.

Nord, E. 1992c. An alternative to the QALY: The Saved Young Life Equivalent (SAVE). *British Medical Journal* 305:875–877.

References

Nord, E. 1993a. The trade-off between severity of illness and treatment effect in cost-value analysis of health care. *Health Policy* 24:227–238.

Nord, E. 1993b. Helsepolitikere ønsker ikke mest mulig helse per krone (Health politicians do not wish to maximize health benefits). *Journal of the Norwegian Medical Association* 113:1171–1173.

Nord, E. 1993c. Unjustified use of the Quality of Well-Being Scale in Oregon. *Health Policy* 24:45–53.

Nord E. 1993d. The relevance of health state after treatment in prioritising between patients. *Journal of Medical Ethics* 19:37–42.

Nord, E. 1993e. Towards quality assurance in QALY-calculations. *International Journal of Technology Assessment in Health Care* 9:37–45.

Nord, E. 1994a. The QALY – a measure of social value rather than individual utility. *Health Economics* 3:89–93.

Nord, E. 1994b. Seminarserie om veiledende verditall for prioritering i helse-vesenet (Workshops on a value table for prioritising in health care). Working paper no. 1/1994. Oslo: National Institute of Public Health.

Nord, E. 1995. The person trade-off approach to valuing health care programs. *Medical Decision Making* 15:201–208.

Nord, E. 1996a. Health status index models for use in resource allocation decisions. A critical review in the light of observed preferences for social choice. *International Journal of Technology Assessment in Health Care* 12:31–44.

Nord, E. 1996b. Time trade-off scores in patients with chronic disease. Comparison with the York hypothetical TTO tariff. Paper for the EuroQol Plenary Meeting, Oslo, October.

Nord, E. 1996c. Veiledende verditall for kostnadnytteanalyser av helsetjenester (A value table for cost-value analysis of health care). Journal of the Norwegian Medical Association 116:3246–3249.

Nord, E.; Pinto, J. L.; Richardson J.; Menzel, P.; and Ubel, P. 1999. Incorporating societal concerns for fairness in numerical valuations of health programmes. *Health Economics* 8:25–39.

Nord, E.; Richardson, J.; and Macarounas-Kirchmann, K. 1993. Social evaluation of health care versus personal evaluation of health states: Evidence on the validity of four health state scaling instruments using Norwegian and Australian surveys. *International Journal of Technology Assessment in Health Care* 9:463–478.

Nord, E.; Richardson, J.; Street, A.; Kuhse, H.; and Singer P. 1995a. Maximising health benefits versus egalitarianism: An Australian survey of health issues. *Social Science & Medicine* 41:1429–1437.

Nord, E.; Richardson, J.; Street, A.; Kuhse, H.; and Singer, P. 1995b. Who cares about cost? Does economic analysis impose or reflect social values? *Health Policy* 34:79–94.

Nord, E.; Street, A.; Richardson, J.; Kuhse, H.; and Singer, P. 1996. The significance of age and duration of effect in social evaluation of health care. *Health Care Analysis* 4:103, 111.

Norwegian Commission for Prioritising in Health Care. 1987. Retningslinjer for prioritering innen helsevesenet (Guidelines for prioritising in health care). Norges offentlige utredninger, 23. Oslo: Universitetsforlaget.

O'Brien, J., and Francis, A. 1988. The use of next-of-kin to estimate pain in cancer patients. *Pain* 35:171–178.

O'Kelly, T. J., and Westaby, S. 1990. Trauma centres and the efficient use of financial resources. *British Journal of Surgery* 77:1142–1144.

O'Leary, J. F.; Fairclough, D. L.; Jankowski, M. K.; and Weeks, J. C. 1995. Comparison of time trade-off utilities and rating scale values of cancer patients and their relatives. *Medical Decision Making* 15:132–137.

Olsen, J. A. 1994. Persons vs years: Two ways of eliciting implicit weights. *Health Economics* 3:39–46.

Olsen, J. A. 1997. Aiding priority setting in health care: Is there a role for the contingent valuation method? *Health Economics* 6:603–612.

Oregon Health Services Commission. 1991. Prioritization of health services. A report to the Governor and Legislature. Salem, Oregon.

Patrick, D. L.; Bush, J. W.; and Chen, M. M. 1973. Methods for measuring levels of well-being for a health status index. *Health Services Research* 8: 228–245.

Pearlman, R. A., and Uhlmann, R. F. 1988. Quality of life in chronic diseases: Perceptions of elderly patients. *Journal of Gerontology* 43:M25–M30.

Pinto, J. L. 1994. The Oregon experience: Scales, numbers and their meaning. Paper for the 14th Spanish Meeting on Health Economics. Santiago de Compostela, June.

Pinto, J. L. 1997. Is the person trade-off a valid method for allocating health care resources? *Health Economics* 6:71–81.

Pinto, J. L., and Perpinan, J. M. A. In press. Health state after treatment: A reason for discrimination?

Rawls, J. 1971. *A theory of justice*. Cambridge, MA: Harvard University Press.

Read, J. L., et al. 1984. Preferences for health outcomes. Comparison of assessment methods. *Medical Decision Making* 4:315–329.

Richardson, J. 1991. Economic assessment of health care: Theory and practice. *The Australian Economic Review* 1st quarter, 4–19.

Richardson, J. 1994. Cost-utility analysis: What should be measured? *Social Science & Medicine* 39:7–21.

Richardson, J. 1997. Critique and some recent contributions to the theory of cost utility analysis. Working paper 77. Melbourne: Centre for Health Program Evaluation.

Richardson, J.; Hall, J.; and Salkeld, G. 1989. Cost utility analysis: The compatibility of measurement techniques and the measurement of utility through time. In C. S. Smith, ed., *Economics and health*: Proceedings of the eleventh Australian conference of health economics.

Richardson, J., and Nord, E. 1997. The importance of perspective in the measurement of quality adjusted life years. *Medical Decision Making* 17:33–41.

Ross, J. 1994. The use of economic evaluation in health care: Australian decision makers' perceptions. *Health Policy* 31:103–110.

Rosser, R.; Cottee, M.; Rabin, R.; and Selai, C. 1992. Index of health-related quality of life. In A. Hopkins, ed., *Measures of the quality of life, and the uses to which they may be put*. London: Royal College of Physicians of London.

Rosser, R., and Kind, P. 1978. A scale of valuations of states of illness: Is there a social consensus? *International Journal of Epidemiology* 7:347–358.

Rothman, M. L., et al. 1991. The validity of proxy-generated scores as measures of patient health status. *Medical Care* 29:115–124.

Rubinstein, L. Z.; Schairer, C.; Wieland, G. D.; and Kane, R. 1984. Systematic biases in functional status assessment of elderly adults: Effects of different data sources. *Journal of Gerontology* 39:686–691.

Sackett, D. L.; Richardson, W. S.; Rosenberg, W.; and Haynes, R. B. 1997. *Evidence based medicine.* New York: Churchill-Livingstone.

Salkeld, G.; Davey, P.; and Arnolda, G. 1995. A critical review of health-related economic evaluations in Australia: Implications for health policy. *Health Policy* 31:111–125.

Schoemaker, P. J. 1982. The expected utility model: Its variants, purposes, evidence and limitations. *Journal of Economic Literature* 20:529–563.

Selai, C., and Rosser, R. 1995. Eliciting EuroQol descriptive data and utility scale values from inpatients. *Pharmacoeconomics* 8:147–158.

Sen, A. 1997. Maximisation and the act of choice. *Econometrica* 65:745–779.

Sherbourne, C.; Sturm, R.; and Wells, K. B. 1997. Development of utility scores for the SF-12. Presentation of the 4th Annual Conference of ISOQOL, Vienna, November. Abstract in *Quality of Life Research* 6 (1997): 721.

Singer, P.; McKie, J.; Kuhse, H.; and Richardson, J. 1995. Double jeopardy and the use of QALYs in health care allocation. *Journal of Medical Ethics* 21: 144–150.

Sintonen, H. 1981. An approach to measuring and valuing health states. *Social Science & Medicine* 15c:55–65.

Sintonen, H. 1994. The 15D-measure of health related quality of life. Reliability, validity and sensitivity of its health state descriptive system. Working paper No. 42. Melbourne: National Centre for Health Program Evaluation.

Sintonen, H., and Pekurinen, M. 1993. A fifteen-dimensional measure of health-related quality of life (15 D) and its applications. In S. R. Walker and R. M. Rosser, eds., *Quality of life assessment: Key issues in the 1990s.* Dordrecht: Kluwer Academic Publishers.

Slevin, M. L., et al. 1988. Who should measure quality of life, the doctor or the patient? *British Journal of Cancer* 57:109–112.

Smith, A. 1987. Qualms about QALYs. *The Lancet* 1:1134–1136.

Smith, G. T. 1990. The economics of hypertension and stroke. *American Heart Journal* 119:725–728.

Spitzer, W. O., et al. 1981. Measuring the quality of life in cancer patients. *Journal of Chronical Disease* 34:585–597.

Stewart, A., et al. 1989. Functional status and well-being of patients with chronic conditions. *JAMA* 262:907–913.

Sutherland, H. J.; Llewellyn-Thomas, H.; Boyd, N. F.; and Till, J. E. 1982. Attitudes toward quality of survival. The concept of "maximum endurable time." *Medical Decision Making* 2:299–309.

Swedish Health Care and Medical Priorities Commission. 1993. No easy choices – the difficulties of health care. Sveriges offentlige utredninger, 93. Stockholm: The Ministry of Health and Social Affairs.

References

Tamura, M.; Kawata, C.; and Hashimoto, M. 1995. An empirical study of the fairness of allocation of health care resources. *Japanese Journal of Health Economics and Policy* 2:55–70 (in Japanese).

Torrance, G. W. 1970. A generalized cost-effectiveness model for the evaluation of health programs. Research report series 101, Faculty of Business, McMaster University, Hamilton.

Torrance, G. W. 1986. Measurement of health state utilities for economic appraisal. *Journal of Health Economics* 5:1–30.

Torrance, G. W. 1987. Utility approach to measuring health related quality of life. *Journal of Chronic Disease* 40:593–600.

Torrance, G. W.; Boyle, M. H.; and Horwood, S. P. 1982. Application of multi-attribute utility theory to measure social preferences for health states. *Operations Research* 30:1043–1069.

Torrance, G. W.; Zhang, Y.; Feeny, D. H.; Furlong, W.; and Barr, R. 1992. Multi-attribute preference functions for a comprehensive health status classification system. Working paper No. 92-18. Hamilton: McMaster University, Centre for Health Economics and Policy Analysis.

Tsevat, J., et al. 1994. Health values of the seriously ill. *Annals of Internal Medicine* 122:514–520.

Tsuchiya, A. 1996. The value of health at different ages. *Journal of Health Care and Society* 6(3) (in Japanese).

Tsuchiya, A. 1997. Should health benefits be age weighted? Paper for UK HESG meeting, January.

Ubel, P. 1997. How stable are people's preferences for giving priority to severely ill patients? Mimeo. Philadelphia, Veterans Affairs Medical Center.

Ubel, P., and Loewenstein, G. 1995. The efficacy and equity of retransplantation: An experimental survey of public attitudes. *Health Policy* 34:145–151.

Ubel, P. A.; Loewenstein, G.; Scanlon, D.; and Kamlet, M. 1996. Individual utilities are inconsistent with rationing choices. *Medical Decision Making* 16:108–116.

Ubel, P; Loewenstein, G; Scanlon, D; and Kamlet, M. 1998. Value measurement in cost-utility analysis: Explaining the difference between rating scale and person trade-off elicitations. *Health Policy* 43:33–44.

Ubel, P.; Nord, E.; Gold, M.; Menzel, P.; Pinto, J. L.; and Richardson, J. In press. Improving value measurement in cost-effectiveness analysis.

Ubel, P.; Spranca, M.; DeKay, M.; Hershey, J.; and Asch, D. A. 1998b. Public preferences for prevention versus cure: What if one ounce of prevention is worth only an ounce of cure? *Medical Decision Making* 18:141–148.

Wagstaff, A. 1991. QALYs and the equity-efficiency trade-off. *Journal of Health Economics* 10:21–41.

Weinstein, M. C. 1981. Economic assessments of medical practices and technologies. *Medical Decision Making* 1:309–330.

Weinstein, M. C., and Stason, W. B. 1977. Foundations of cost-effectiveness analysis for health analysis and medical practices. *New England Journal of Medicine* 296:716–721.

Williams, A. 1981. Welfare economics and health status measurement. In J. van der Gaag and M. Perlman, eds., *Health, economics and health economics.* Amsterdam: North Holland Publishing Company.

Williams, A. 1985. Economics of coronary artery bypass grafting. *British Medical Journal* 291:326–329.

Williams, A. 1987a. Who is to live? A question for the economist or the doctor? *World Hospitals* 13:34–45.

Williams, A. 1987b. Response: QALYfying the value of life. *Journal of Medical Ethics* 13:123.

Williams, A. 1988a. The measurement and valuations of improvements in health. University of York, Centre for Health Economics. Newsletter 3/1988.

Williams, A. 1988b. Ethics and efficiency in the provision of health care. In J. M. Bell and S. Mendus, eds., *Philosophy and Medical Welfare.* Cambridge University Press.

Williams, A. 1988c. Health economics: The end of clinical freedom? *British Medical Journal* 297:1183–1186.

Williams, A. 1994. Economics, Society and Health Care Ethics. In R. Gillon, ed., *Principles of health care ethics.* London: John Wiley & Sons.

Williams, A. 1995a. The role for the EuroQol Instrument in QALY calculations. Discussion paper 130. York: Centre for Health Economics.

Williams, A. 1995b. The measurement and valuation of health: A chronicle. Discussion paper 136. York: Centre for Health Economics.

Williams, A. 1997. Intergenerational equity: An exploration of the "fair innings" argument. *Health Economics* 6:117–132.

World Bank. 1993. *World development report 1993: Investing in health.* New York: Oxford University Press.

Yager, J., and Linn, L. S. 1981. Physician-patient agreement about depression: Notation in medical records. *General Hospital Psychiatry* 3:271–276.

Index